Malcolm X

A Biography

Author: Jalen Thomas

Table Of Contents

Table Of Contents

Introduction

Chapter 1: The Early Life of Malcolm Little

    The Death of Earl Little

    A Family Breaks Down

        A Mother's Insanity

Chapter 2: A New Life

Chapter 3: A Young Man With Wide Eyes

    First Steps in Boston

    Another View of the World

    Detroit Red

    Robbery, Arrest, and Prison

Chapter 4: In a Cell, a New Malcolm is Born

    The Nation of Islam

        The Nation of Islam's Main Beliefs

        A List of Demands From the Nation of Islam

    Malcolm Adds the X

Chapter 5: The Start of Malcolm X and the Nation of Islam

    Birth of a New Nation of Islam Minister

Chapter 6: Malcolm X and the Nation of Islam

   Slavery Was A Prophecy in the Bible

   Nation of Islam Beliefs on Race

   Why Malcolm X and the Civil Rights Movement Didn't Mix at First

Chapter 7: Malcolm Helps the Nation of Islam Grow

Chapter 8: Malcolm the Family Man

Chapter 9: Malcolm's Rise Into the Spotlight

   The Hate that Hate Produced

   Malcolm's Surprise from the White Race

   Hinton Johnson Event

   More Malcolm in the Late 1950s

Chapter 10: Departure from the Nation of Islam

   Muhammad Doesn't Support Malcolm's Decision

   A Different Side to Elijah Muhammad

   Kennedy's Assassination, the Nation of Islam, and Malcolm X

   Malcolm's Split from the Nation of Islam

Chapter 11: Life After the Nation of Islam

   Change of Views

   Malcolm's Organizations

      Muslim Mosque, Inc.

      Organization of Afro-American Unity

Journey to Mecca

Malcolm Continues his Travels

Africa

Malcolm's Return to the United States

Chapter 12: Murder of an Icon

Reactions to the Death of a Controversial Civil Rights Advocate

Conspiracy Theories

Chapter 13: How Malcolm's Reputation Changed

Chapter 14: Malcolm's Legacy Continues Today

Films and Books

Malcolm's Memorials and Tributes

Conclusion

Bibliography

Introduction

"I am not a racist. I am against every form of racism and segregation, every form of discrimination. I believe in human beings, and that all human beings should be respected as such, regardless of their color." — Malcolm X[1]

During the civil rights movement of the 1950s and 1960s, many people called Malcolm X "the angriest black man in America" due to his acceptance of violence.[2] Malcolm X believed that if violence changed the treatment of African Americans, then it was the answer. This was a drastic change from the way other civil rights groups handled protesting, mainly because Martin Luther King Jr. felt the opposite way Malcolm X felt.

This book will not only detail Malcolm X's life during the civil rights era; it will be a story of his life from beginning to end. This book will not only highlight Malcolm X's achievements but his challenges, his transformations, and his beliefs and wishes. The book will take a deeper look into the man that everyone started to know as "the angriest man in America." The book will look at why Malcolm X was so angry at the world by the time he reached the civil rights era, a time he looked forward to as a child, where he and every other African American would receive equality in America. A view that started to completely change in his adult life as he began to feel that this equality would never be achieved in America.

---

[1] Malcolmx.com. (n.d.). Quotes – Malcolm X. [online] Available at: http://www.malcolmx.com/quotes/.

[2] Akinti, P. (2005). Malcolm X insulted. [online] the Guardian. Available at: https://www.theguardian.com/world/2005/may/26/usa.features11.

This book is a narrative biography with information gathered from other biographies and Malcolm X's autobiography, *The Autobiography of Malcolm X,* and in-depth research on the civil rights movement and the Nation of Islam, which was a big part of Malcolm X's life. Through this information, I have created a narrative biography on Malcolm X in a way that the world can get to know him as more than just the angry African American man who preached about ending segregation towards African Americans through any means possible, including violence.

This book will bring you through Malcolm's life-changing journey that brought him to the last year of his life. After leaving the Nation of Islam in the early 1960s, Malcolm traveled to Mecca, the ultimate goal for Muslims. During this journey, Malcolm realized what he thought was impossible throughout his life was, in fact, possible. After believing since he was a young child that African Americans and white Americans could not live side by side equally, Malcolm looked at the crowd after his journey and saw people of all races coming together for one cause. After this experience, Malcolm focused the rest of his life to speaking to crowds about coming together as one nation in order to overcome the problems the United States holds with racism.

Malcolm X's childhood and life experiences molded him into the man who went from being called Malcolm Little to Malcolm X and then, towards the end of his life, Malcolm X Shabazz. Therefore, if we don't delve into the whole life of Malcolm X, we will never be able to truly know the man behind the name.

Throughout this book, you will see a variety of quotes from Malcolm X. No matter how people felt about Malcolm X during his lifetime or now, you can't deny the brilliance

Malcolm X had while he spoke to large crowds and how he was able to persuade them about his beliefs and the beliefs of the Nation of Islam. Through these speeches, Malcolm X provided insight into his beliefs and what he felt the people of the United States could and couldn't achieve. Malcolm X's own words will give you a more in-depth look into the man himself. □

Chapter 1: The Early Life of Malcolm Little

Malcolm Little, the person who would become Malcolm X and later Malcolm X Shabazz, came into this world on May 19, 1925. He joined his parents and three siblings in their Omaha, Nebraska, home. Malcolm's father, Earl Little, supported Marcus Garvey, who was an early civil rights activist while working as a Baptist minister and carpenter. His mother, Louise Helen Little, worked as a branch reporter and secretary of the Universal Negro Improvement Association (UNIA). Louise sent the local UNIA news to a newspaper based in New York City called the *Negro World*. The *Negro World* was the universal newspaper for the UNIA, both of which Marcus Garvey established in 1910.

From Malcolm's first day in this world, he was surrounded by African Americans who strove to create a better life for themselves and future generations but often were held back by prejudice. While Malcolm would grow up with parents who not only taught him to stand up for himself and not fear the white population, which most African Americans did during Malcolm's childhood, Malcolm would also see the dangers of standing up for equality. Malcolm learned early that the white man was a danger to African Americans as white supremacist groups killed most of his father's brothers and his father. However, through his parents installing black pride and independence into him and his siblings, Malcolm became ready to take on the world in a way no one, not even his parents or siblings, ever imagined.

The Death of Earl Little

During the civil rights movement, Malcolm X became known for his belief that you should be willing to die for what you believe in. This is a belief Malcolm received from his father, who died fighting for what he believed in, which was not only creating a better life for his family but for all African Americans.

A year after Malcolm's birth, the family moved to Milwaukee, Wisconsin, due to threats they received from the Ku Klux Klan. One night, while Earl was at work, the KKK came and swarmed around the Little's house, yelling for Earl to show himself. Instead, Louisa went out to tell the Klan that he wasn't home. They then told Louise that they weren't going to allow her husband to continue to spread his word around their community. Malcolm discusses this event and the family's move to Wisconsin in more detail in Alex Haley's *The Autobiography of Malcolm X*.[3] Malcolm states that he never understood why his father decided to move the family because of the threats from the KKK.

Not too long after, the family again relocated, this time making their home in Lansing, Michigan. The reasoning behind this move was that Earl wanted the family to be able to raise their own food. He also had dreams of one day starting a business and felt that Wisconsin wouldn't be the right place for his dreams. Unfortunately, the harassment from racist groups followed the Little family as Lansing, Michigan, was home to the Black Legion, a white supremacist group. The Black Legion targeted the Little family because they lived outside of the

---

[3] X, M. and Haley, A. (1965). The Autobiography of Malcolm X. New York: Random House Publishing Group. Kindle Edition.

African American community and Earl was in the process of getting his business up and running. Earl became more of a target when he started to preach to other African Americans in the community. Like the KKK, the Black Legion didn't want any trouble from the African Americans and they felt Earl wanted trouble.

When the Little's home burned down in 1929, Earl blamed the Black Legion. Malcolm discussed this night as one of his earliest memories, stating he was quickly snatched out of bed.[4] He remembered his father shooting at a couple of white men, who were running away from their burning house. Of course, this accusation didn't sit well with members of the Black Legion, and they furthered their efforts to cause trouble with the Little family.

Malcolm's world turned upside down at the age of six when his father died. While authorities ruled Earl's death as accidental, Louise wasn't convinced. She believed that the Black Legion murdered her husband. For little Malcolm, this event traumatized him. While he never learned the truth to his father's death, he did learn racism could take someone's life, and this realization only grew as he learned about his uncles who were also killed by white supremacist groups. Near the end of his life, Malcolm X met with author Alex Haley with plans to write Malcolm's autobiography. As he spoke to Haley, Malcolm became very open of his life, his views, and the situations that molded him into becoming Malcolm X. During the conversation, Malcolm told Haley that he truly believed a white supremacist group murdered his father. Though at the time, their family's biggest threat was the Black Legion, Malcolm also stated that it could have easily been the Ku Klux Klan. While the Black Legion wore black and the KKK were

---

[4] Ibid.

known for their white uniforms, Malcolm knew that both groups stood for the same principles and despised his father and not only threatened his life but the lives of his whole family.

A Family Breaks Down

After the death of Earl, Louise struggled to care for her family. While Louise did whatever she could, including renting out part of her garden and heading to the welfare office, to keep a roof over their head, it never seemed to be enough. Malcolm and his siblings didn't always have enough food, which caused them to start stealing food so that they wouldn't starve.

During this time, Malcolm started to feel embarrassed about his family's poverty. While he lived in an area where the majority of African American families lived in poverty, it became well-known that the Little family was the poorest family in the area. This bothered Malcolm both mentally and emotionally. While he was young and didn't truly understand the meaning of poverty and his family's situation, Malcolm hated the fact that in order to not starve, they often had to steal food. But soon, Malcolm's frustration took over and he became a regular thief. Soon, this behavior turned towards other areas of Malcolm's life, such as school. A young boy who once showed promise as a great student started to show poor grades and an attitude where he didn't care about school.

Over time, Malcolm started to notice a change in his mother and, as he grew, he started to blame the people from the Seventh Day Adventist Church, who Louise had befriended. They would often invite the family over to eat and discuss their religion. While Louise became very active in their religious activities, her children, especially Malcolm, didn't feel the same way. However, the children went and often listened to what they had to say because it became a way for them to get a good home-cooked meal.

During the same time that Louise started to become an active member of the Seventh Day Adventist church, the county welfare office started to visit the family. While Louise argued with them about how they couldn't come into her house, they insisted they could as they had to talk to the children, and they had the law on their side. Feeling defeated, she continued to let them in. Later in his life, Malcolm remembered these interviews with the welfare people and stated that he believed they were trying to plant seeds into the minds of him and his siblings. Malcolm, who was the first target for the welfare people because he was more mischievous than his other siblings, felt that the welfare office thought they needed to send the children into foster care. To Malcolm, the welfare agency acted like it was their responsibility to take the children out of the home because they weren't cared for in the home. Of course, because Malcolm had been caught stealing, they often used him as a reason when telling Louise that she didn't care for her children properly.

The last straw for the family's unity occurred when welfare workers told the children, in front of Louise, that she was crazy because she refused to take pork from their neighbor. Most of the children understood they didn't eat pork because their religion didn't allow it. However, they also knew that they had very little food and were hungry most of the time. The children were already torn about their mother rejecting free meat while they starved and then welfare workers, people who were held in certain authority by the children, told them that their mother was crazy because she refused the pork. Near the end of his life, Malcolm stated that if the welfare workers would have left the family alone, they could've made it through the tough times, even if Malcolm caused so much stress and trouble. But, because the welfare workers acted as they did, planting seeds to try to split the family apart to make their jobs of separating them easier, the family began to fall apart.

Not too long after this event, the welfare workers started to look for other homes for the children. They began this process with Malcolm because he was the one they stated was different from the other children. Upon talking to the Gohannas family, who knew the Little family, they agreed to take in Malcolm. When the welfare workers came to inform Louise of the plans for the Gohannas family to take in Malcolm, she refused. Malcolm, on the other hand, didn't fully see a problem with it as his family was falling apart and he was tired of his homelife situation.

But instead of Malcolm going to live with the Gohannas family, he started to see an African American man visit the house regularly. The children soon learned that their mother and this man were a couple as every time he came over, Louise would dress up nice. Malcolm also began to realize that Louise hoped to get rid of the welfare people if she had a man in her life. Not only would he bring in extra income, but he would also be able to help discipline the children, which was an area that Louise struggled with. The relationship lasted around a year. One day the man was at their house, and the next day he was never seen or heard from again.

A Mother's Insanity

This was when Louise completely started to lose touch with reality. Her interest in her eight children became less and less and soon the children started noticing other erratic behavior from their mother, such as talking to herself. It didn't take long for the welfare workers to realize that Louise was losing touch with reality and they quickly acted on removing the children from the home, starting with Malcolm. At first, they started to drop hints that Malcolm would enjoy living with the Gohannas family because they were such nice people and were looking forward to taking care of him. While Malcolm liked the Gohannas family, he didn't want to leave his brothers and sisters as he felt a responsibility to his young siblings, especially Reginald, who was a sickly child and looked up to him. He also looked up to his older brother and sister, who were more of his parents than his siblings. However, the day came when one of the welfare people came to take Malcolm to the Gohannas family. By this time, Louise had become more and more unresponsive, didn't keep up the house, and barely kept up with her children, so Malcolm, while he would miss his siblings, was a little relieved of his change of homelife.

For a while, the Gohannas family, specifically Big Boy, would bring Malcolm to his mother's house to visit with her and his siblings. Over time, he started to notice his mother declining more and more, and soon, the welfare people were finding homes for his other siblings as well. By 1938, Louise talked to herself continuously and could no longer care for any of her children as she suffered a complete nervous breakdown. At that moment, all the court orders were signed, and in 1939, Louise became a patient at the Kalamazoo State Mental Hospital.

Later in his life, Malcolm discussed seeing his mother in the hospital and how, when he went to see her in the early 1950s, she couldn't remember who he was, and he couldn't believe the state she was in. Louise would remain in the Kalamazoo State Mental Hospital until 1963 when Malcolm, along with his brothers and sisters, were able to get her released. She then lived with Malcolm's brother Philbert and his wife until she passed away.

Chapter 2: A New Life

The little kids continued to stay in contact with each other as often as they could, which was usually during school. At the time, Malcolm was thirteen years old and didn't care too much about school. One day, after causing too much trouble in class, Malcolm was expelled. While he thought he would be able to stay with the Gohannas family, authorities proved him wrong when they came to pick him up to go to another family. But before he went to go live with another family, he was going to spend some time in a reform school.

On the day Malcolm went to the reform school, Mr. Allen picked him up. Later in his life, Malcolm recalled Mr. Allen as one of the nicest welfare people he ever knew. As they were leaving, Mr. Allen turned to the Gohannases and a couple of others who were crying as they were leaving and spoke comforting words. While they were on their way to the reform school in Mason, Michigan, Mr. Allen explained to Malcolm that this wasn't a school for bad children as so many people believed. He stated that it was a home where kids like Malcolm could go and get on the right path to become successful adults. Mr. Allen then told Malcolm that his grades showed he could become successful if he just put effort into it.

The teenage Malcolm became well-liked by the couple who ran the group home. The Swerlins, owners of the group home, gave Malcolm the confidence and care he needed to turn his life around. He started focusing more on his studies and realized he didn't have to steal to get what he needed. Instead, he started to learn that hard work and dedication would help lead him to success.

It was at the detention home with the Swerlins where Malcolm started to notice the difference between white and black people. While he noticed everyone could get along and be kind to one another, he also learned that food prepared by white folk tasted different than the food he was used to. He also noted that they smelled different. Malcolm's time with the Swerlins would change his life in many ways. Not only would he realize that he could become successful if he put his mind to it, but he also realized the beliefs white people, such as the Swerlins, had about African Americans. While they treated him well, Malcolm noticed they still felt that he wasn't a human being like they were. These realizations would come back to Malcolm as an adult when they would become the basis for some of his beliefs during the civil rights era.

Unfortunately, no matter how hard Malcolm worked, many people would still push him away from his goals and dreams. One of these people was his English teacher, Mr. Ostrowski, who asked Malcolm what he wanted to be when he grew up. Malcolm replied that he had dreams of becoming a lawyer. Because he had higher grades than several of his classmates, he felt he could become a successful lawyer. But Mr. Ostrowski told Malcolm his career dreams weren't realistic as most law schools didn't accept African Americans.

Hearing these words shocked and confused Malcolm. He couldn't understand why he would be turned away from a school just because of the color of his skin. These words also became a turning point in Malcolm's life. While he had known about the inequalities and injustices African Americans faced in the United States, especially after the death of his father, he had no idea how strong the racism and prejudice against African Americans were until that moment.

From then on, Malcolm started to change from the boy who

worked hard so he could become successful to the man who wanted nothing more than to be considered equal as a human being. In school and at the detention home, Malcolm started to withdraw. He did what he was told, went to class, and continued to work his odd jobs at the detention home, such as washing dishes. However, Malcolm also started to react to the derogatory terms African American heard daily. People started to discuss Malcolm's change in behavior as he would glare at those who talked down about African Americans.

It wasn't too long after his change in behavior that the Swerlins told him their home wasn't the right fit for him anymore. Mrs. Swerlin told Malcolm that he was to go live with the Lyons family as she couldn't help him if he wouldn't tell her why he was so unhappy. Malcolm assured Mrs. Swerlin that nothing was wrong, gathered his things, and went with Mr. Allen to his new home.

Similar to what Mrs. Swerlin tried to do for weeks before Malcolm went to go live with the Lyons, they, too, continued to ask him what was wrong. They were another family who enjoyed Malcolm and were happy to have him in their home as they wanted to try to help him just like Mr. and Mrs. Swerlin tried.

Chapter 3: A Young Man With Wide Eyes

Malcolm only stayed with the Lyons family for a couple of months, basically to finish his eighth-grade education. During his stay with the Lyons, he met up with his siblings and spoke to Ella, his older sister who had moved to Boston, about wanting to go live with her. Ella quickly acted upon Malcolm's request and at the end of the school year, he boarded a bus heading to Boston.

First Steps in Boston

Later in his life, Malcolm noted that his move to Boston after his junior high years became extremely essential in his life. He was very adamant that if he would've stayed in Michigan, he would've settled for one of the African American girls he liked, gotten married, and started a family. In a sense, Malcolm was stating that he would've never become Malcolm X if he'd stayed in Michigan. It was his move to Boston which started to mold the man who would be written in the history books as Malcolm X.

When Malcolm reached Boston, life became a whole new world from him. With his sister Ella's help, he soon learned the ins and outs of Boston living, including the way people dressed. As Malcolm learned, he soon saw a whole new world for the way African Americans lived. While Boston still had poor African American communities, he also came across many African Americans who lived better than any he had seen in his time in Michigan.

At the time, Malcolm saw African Americans who were not only successful but seemed to snobbishly turn away from poor African Americans. Of course, later in his life, Malcolm changed his tune about the successful African Americans he met in Boston, more specifically in an area of Boston known as Roxbury. Instead of seeing them as a different type of African American, he simply saw them as more successful than the African Americans he knew in Michigan. He also came to realize that just like the African Americans he knew in Michigan, these African Americans had been brainwashed, just in a different way. Instead of being the brainwashed Christian African Americans he had known in Michigan, the Roxbury African American community took pride in their success and the knowledge that they were better than lower-class African Americans. Malcolm came to realize that what the Roxbury African Americans were really doing was imitating the white people he knew in Michigan. Nevertheless, they were not better than other African Americans, no matter how much they believed they were.

Despite Ella's wishes for Malcolm to start meeting and hanging out with the African American boys his age from Roxbury, Malcolm turned to the ghetto part of the area, where he felt more comfortable. While there, he met a group of people and got a job as a shoe shiner. One of the men he started to hang out with was known as Shorty, who had also grown up in the Lansing, Michigan. Through this life, Malcolm became involved in the dance world, where he quickly learned that white women would go to African American dance halls, but African Americans weren't allowed in white dance halls. He also quickly learned that the majority of white women at

23

African American dances were prostitutes who were brought by their pimps. It didn't take too long for Malcolm to start getting his first taste of alcohol, drugs, and women.

Another View of the World

Over the course of a few years, Malcolm continued to work odd jobs and hang out with Shorty and others, including a few girlfriends. While Ella didn't fully approve of Malcolm's choice of friends, she continued to support him and hoped that one day he would become one of the successful African Americans in Roxbury. However, at the age of sixteen, Malcolm had other thoughts and took a job working for the railroad as he wanted to set his feet in the city of New York.

In order to get the railroad job, Malcolm had to lie about his age. Though he was only sixteen years old, he told them he was twenty-one. Receiving a job as kitchen staff, Malcolm started to work for the railroad. He had planned everything out and, providing his plans worked out, he would be able to continue to see his girlfriend, Sophia, who Ella didn't approve of, and work for the railroad so that he could travel. But instead of sending him traveling right away, the railroad put Malcolm to work loading food onto the train cars. He then learned that the job he had been promised, which was the fourth cook, was more of a dishwasher. While Malcolm became a bit disappointed over this realization, he quickly got over it as all he really wanted was to travel and see other parts of the United States.

When Malcolm did reach the city of New York and later, Washington, he worked hard during the day and then spent his time sightseeing at night. One of the most memorable moments during Malcolm's time working on the railroad happened when he visited Washington, D.C. Not only did he see Capitol Hill, but not too far from one of the most famous areas of the United States was the poorest African American community he had ever seen. He couldn't believe that families lived in shacks with dirt floors, children ran around late at night without socks or shoes, begging for pennies, and the crime was higher than any he had seen before. In fact, before he went out, several of his coworkers warned Malcolm that he needed to be very careful in that area because robberies, stabbings, and shootings happened all the time. But the most surprising part of this for Malcolm was that these crimes happened between African Americans and not between whites and African Americans.

One day Malcolm made it to Harlem, a place he had heard about so many times from his dad. A place his father had spoken highly about, and he had only dreamed of one day going. But no matter what people told Malcolm about Harlem, nothing could prepare him to really see the community. One of the places that stuck in Malcolm's mind was a little bar called Small's Paradise. Before Malcolm even walked in, he became amazed that an African American owned the business as it was a huge building and looked even nicer inside. He also noticed that the African Americans in Harlem acted differently than the ones he knew in Michigan or met in Boston. They had a more conservative nature, and instead of making noise and partying when they drank, they sat quietly and talked to each other. Malcolm quickly noticed that they all seemed to know each other, especially the bartender, who knew what most of them drank and would have it in front of them before they even sat down.

Another point Malcolm noticed was that they never flashed their money around. Instead, they took it out of their wallet, paid the bartender, and put it away. Malcolm stated in Haley's *Autobiography of Malcolm X* that he had never seen any African Americans react that way with money before as they always flashed around whatever money they had.[5] Even though Malcolm quickly learned that the African Americans he saw in Small's Paradise were a small percentage of the African Americans in Harlem, he had new inspiration. He also quickly learned that Harlem was full of the loud African Americans he knew so well.

Malcolm continued to work for the railroad until he was fired during the early 1940s. He then traveled back to Michigan to see his brothers and sisters, who he hadn't seen since he left as a young teenage boy. Once he returned to Boston, he realized that the only thing he knew was the railroad and soon sought another railroad job. At this time, World War II had been going on for two years, and America had joined the war a couple of months before, after the bombing of Pearl Harbor. Of course, at the age of seventeen, many people, including Malcolm, were well aware that he could be drafted for the war.

In 1943, Malcolm moved to Harlem, where he continued his life of random jobs, gambling, and started to get involved with crime. Not too long after his Harlem move, he received his draft notice for the war. He quickly came up with an insane idea so that he wouldn't be sent off to war. Malcolm repeated the following statement several times: "I want to be sent down South. Organize them nigger soldiers ... steal us some guns, and kill us some crackers."[6] After evaluation, the army stated he wasn't mentally suited for enlistment.

---

[5] X, M. and Haley, A. (1965). The Autobiography of Malcolm X. New York: Random House Publishing Group. Kindle Edition.

Detroit Red

While Malcolm lived in Harlem as a late teen and into his early twenties, he gained the nickname "Detroit Red." The reason for the nickname was simple. Malcolm came from Lansing, Michigan, but because most of his crowd in Harlem had never heard of a city called Lansing before, Malcolm started to say he lived near Detroit. Malcolm gained the nickname "Red" before the word Detroit was added to it because when he came to Harlem, he looked like a typical Midwest person, reminding the crowd of a redneck. Malcolm stated that once they gave him the nickname Detroit Red, it stuck, and he became forever known by that name to that crowd of people. Even when he went to prison and later converted to the Nation of Islam religion, he didn't hang out or see that crowd much, but they still referred to him as Detroit Red.

Later in Malcolm's life, he came to feel that Detroit Red was one of his personas. Detroit Red was the young African American kid who had just left the Midwest to go live with his sister in the big city of New York because he couldn't stand the reform school he was in because his teacher told him he could never be an attorney, which was his career aspiration. He was the kid who was lost and trying to find himself in a new state and culture, one who opened his eyes to the different ways African Americans lived. He was that kid that could have gone back to school and stayed in the middle-class part of Harlem but decided to find the location where he felt most comfortable, the area of Harlem which reminded him of home. Even though this kid hung out in a bar and gambled away

[6] X, M. and Haley, A. (1965). The Autobiography of Malcolm X. New York: Random House Publishing Group. Kindle Edition.

most of the money he earned from odd jobs, he was decently happy and enjoyed the group of friends he found.

For Malcolm, Detroit Red was the person that sent him to prison for a number of years. Then, once he found the Nation of Islam and started writing regularly to the religious organization's leader, Elijah Muhammad, Detroit Red left, and Malcolm X took his place. Throughout Malcolm's life, people would come to realize that with every major transformation, he changed a part of his name. While some names, such as Detroit Red, were given to him, most of them, such as Malcolm X, were ones that he created for himself. He would go through another name change when he left the Nation of Islam almost a decade after he joined.

Robbery, Arrest, and Prison

A couple of years after moving to Harlem, Malcolm found himself on the wrong side of the law. While in Boston during 1945, Malcolm joined Shorty and a few other people and started a series of robberies. Their targets were wealthy white families and these robberies went on for a few months. It wasn't until February 1946 when authorities caught and arrested Malcolm, Shorty, and the others.

When the group got in front of the judge, there were about twenty-one charges between them. Malcolm received a sentence of ten years in prison. Handcuffed together with Shorty, the group made their way to Charlestown State Prison. By this time, Malcolm was a strong atheist and only twenty-one years old. He wasn't sure what prison held for him, but he soon learned.

Of course, one of the first situations Malcolm had to deal with was withdrawal. For years, Malcolm had lived in a nearly constant flow of alcohol and drugs and, now in prison, he had none in his system. He became angry and physically miserable for many reasons. Not only did he deal with withdrawal, but he also dealt with the prison's cramped and dirty cells. But, for Malcolm, the worst part became the bars. He hated feeling like a caged animal.

Malcolm came to a lot of realizations while behind the bars of his jail cell. It was during this time that Malcolm learned the true meaning of being in a cage. This also became a time when Malcolm would go from hating the world to finding one of the callings in his life, public speaking.

Chapter 4: In a Cell, a New Malcolm is Born

Malcolm started to change his behavior about a year after being in prison. One of the men Malcolm always credited with helping him find his way was John Bembry, who was another convict. Bembry quickly noted Malcolm's intelligence and soon took him under his wing. Malcolm was in awe of Bembry because he had never met a man who commanded such respect just by the use of words. Bembry showed Malcolm a whole new world with reading, one that helped him pass the time in prison. Malcolm quickly began picking up one book after the other and soon became more interested in attaining an education.

Bembry wasn't the only person who was trying to change Malcolm's life around. A few of his siblings back in Michigan begin to write him a series of letters, all expressing an interest in a rising religious movement known as the Nation of Islam.

The Nation of Islam

The Nation of Islam, more commonly known as NOI, was started on July 4, 1930, by a man named Wallace D. Fard Muhammad in Detroit, Michigan. The goals of the religious movement were to improve the lives of African Americans with a focus on their economic, spiritual, social, and mental conditions. Malcolm's siblings quickly realized this form of black pride was something that would interest Malcolm, and they were correct. However, Malcolm didn't pick up interest in the Nation of Islam at first. In fact, it wasn't until his brother, Reginald, sent Malcolm a letter and told him he could help Malcolm get out of prison, but first, he needed to stop eating pork and smoking cigarettes, that Malcolm became interested.

Malcolm, who despised being behind bars, took Reginald up on his offer and immediately stopped smoking and eating pork. It wasn't long after that when Reginald came to visit and had a one-on-one conversation with Malcolm about the Nation of Islam. After this conversation, Malcolm started to look more closely into the African American political and religious movement. It was during this time when Malcolm started to believe that every conversation and relationship he'd held throughout his life with a white person had been full of greed, dishonesty, and hatred. He then began to see the white population as devils, which was exactly what the Nation of Islam taught. Malcolm became even more interested in the Nation of Islam when he realized they were discussing African Americans moving back to Africa in order to become totally free from whites. This idea wasn't new to Malcolm or his siblings as their father had believed the same thing.

Malcolm, who had come to gain the nickname of Satan in prison due to his atheist beliefs and angry personality, started to change his tune and over time, he started to believe in the ways of the Nation of Islam and thought about converting.

Before he converted to the Nation of Islam, Malcolm wrote a letter to Elijah Muhammad, who was the leader of the religious movement in 1948. In the letter, Malcolm asked Muhammad for advice on converting, inquired about the beliefs of the Nation of Islam, explained a bit about his life, such as where he was and why, and asked what to do. When

Malcolm received Muhammad's reply, the leader told Malcolm to pray. Malcolm, who had been an atheist for years, admitted to struggling to bring himself to pray at first. However, he eventually bent his knees and started the prayer. From that moment on, Malcolm continued to not only pray but to preach prayer.

The Nation of Islam's Main Beliefs

When Malcolm became a part of the Nation of Islam, especially when he requested the role of minister and Muhammad approved, Malcolm had to follow everything the Nation of Islam believed in, at least outwardly. While he followed these beliefs at first, over time, they started to change, and he either started to twist these beliefs into his own or stopped believing them in general. However, it's important to note that whenever Malcolm spoke about what members of the Nation of Islam were supposed to believe, he started the statement with "Elijah Muhammad says." Today, many historians and biographers of Malcolm X believed he did this on purpose because he didn't fully believe in what he was preaching, but because of his excellent talent with public speaking, he could draw a crowd, keep their attention, and speak with passion.

Before we get too far into Malcolm X and his world with the Nation of Islam, it's important to understand the beliefs and principles of this religious organization. For a large part of his life, Malcolm spent his time preaching the beliefs of the Nation of Islam. These same beliefs are described below.

According to the Nation of Islam website and a book titled *Message to the Blackman in America*, written by the National of Islam leader at the time, Elijah Muhammad, published in 1965, the organization has a dozen basic beliefs.

First, the members of the Nation of Islam believe there is only one true God. To them, the name of God is Allah. This belief became a very staple point within Malcolm's teachings in front of his congregation and in his speeches in front of the world. He often discussed Allah and thanked Allah for all the blessings in his life.

Second, the Nation of Islam believes in the scriptures of the Holy Qur'an and in all of Allah's prophets. When it came to the Nation of Islam during Malcolm's time with them, you didn't question the holy book or the organization's leader, Elijah Muhammad. Some historians and others who have studied Malcolm believe that this could be one of the reasons he changed his views or when he didn't always follow the rules, did it as quietly as he could. Malcolm also studied the Qur'an throughout his time as a member of the Nation of Islam. In fact, this was one of the books Malcolm read while he was in prison that helped convince him to become a member of the organization.

Third, while the Nation of Islam believes in the Bible, they also believe they need to reinterpret this holy book because people have messed with the messages in the Bible. They believe that the pieces that have been added to the Bible are false, and they do not want to be tricked into believing the words of humanity over the words of Allah.

In the fourth belief, the Nation of Islam basically states that what is stated in the scriptures and what Allah's prophets said is the truth as they received this information from Allah's prophets.

The fifth belief discusses resurrection and how African Americans will be the first to receive resurrection because they are the ones who need resurrection the most. When it comes to resurrection, the Nation of Islam believes in mental resurrection and not physical. This belief is very important to some of Malcolm's central thoughts in his speeches because he often discussed how the African American race is superior to the white race. This belief's basis is nearly the same as the belief that states that African Americans are more fitting to be chosen by God than anyone else because African American are more righteous and will not be rejected by God like other races in America. Just as many other religions believe, the Nation of Islam believes that God picks who will be resurrected, and who won't be, by their actions and how good they are.

Sixth, the Nation of Islam believes that God will come to the United States to make his first judgment, just as is stated in the holy book. The members of the Nation of Islam didn't worry about this judgment day during Malcolm's time because they believed they would be chosen by God first as they were the superior race and more deserving of his praise. This belief also ties closely into all of Malcolm's remarks about African Americans being the superior race.

The seventh belief discusses true African American freedom and separation by white Americans. The members of the Nation of Islam during Malcolm's time believed that it was time for them to gain their true independence after all their bondage and segregation history in America. However, this belief didn't just mean physical separation, as it also talked about freeing of their last names, as the last names of African Americans were generally the last names of their ancestors' slave owners. To truly create freedom from the grips of white America, African Americans needed to take their true last names back, the names of their people and not the people that had held their families in bondage. Nearly every member of the Nation of Islam during Malcolm's time followed this rule by adding an "x" to their name. Malcolm became known as Malcolm X because his last name of Little was his ancestor's slave owner's name and he could not start his road to true freedom without letting go of his last name.

The eighth belief discusses equality and justice for African Americans, which was a central theme in Malcolm's work as a minister for the Nation of Islam and also as a civil and human rights advocate near the end of his life. However, when Malcolm started to change his tune near the end of his life, he stopped saying that the African American race was above the white race due to what he saw once he completed his pilgrimage to Mecca. But the Nation of Islam believed their race was superior to the white race because they didn't believe that they could be equal to the race which held their people in bondage for so long. However, the eighth belief doesn't end with this. There is a little disclaimer between the eighth and ninth belief which states that the members of the Nation of Islam respect and recognize that all American citizens are independent, and they respect the American laws which govern the country.

The ninth belief of the Nation of Islam once again discusses separation between African Americans and the white people of America. This belief ties into the civil rights movement as it stated that the members of the Nation of Islam don't believe that African Americans and white American citizens can ever live in harmony in America. Instead, the members of the Nation of Islam believe that this is a trap and is a plan to help keep them in the country because the white Americans realize that African Americans want to leave to go back to their homeland. They further state that it's not possible to forget about hundreds of years of white Americans and African

Americans living as enemies and suddenly becoming friends because white Americans want to integrate with African Americans. Instead of allowing integration to happen, the members of the Nation of Islam want to preach the point that history should prove integration can't happen and African Americans need to separate completely from white Americans and start their own nation. The belief continues to state that if white American really want to integrate, they can start by allowing African Americans to work. And by this, the members of the Nation of Islam don't mean let a few African Americans work, but they want the white Americans to find work for every single unemployed African American. But the Nation of Islam also states that they know this is impossible because there just isn't enough work for all the millions of unemployed African Americans.

The tenth belief of the Nation of Islam deals with wars. The members of the Nation of Islam don't participate in wars which take human life. Because of all the drafts in American history, which more than likely affected many members of the Nation of Islam, their beliefs state that they shouldn't have to participate in these wars. They have nothing they can get from the United States, so they don't believe they should have to send their people over to fight in wars where they will gain nothing from the country. In the end, the Nation of Islam leader does state that his members will fight in American wars if they can gain territory, so they can feel they have something to fight for.

The eleventh belief talks about African American women, specifically the women who are part of the Nation of Islam religious organization. But many members still focus on protecting women whether they are members or not. This belief states that African American women shouldn't be disrespected and need to be protected just as any other women from other nations are. This belief was very close to Malcolm's staple beliefs and was something he often discussed. It's also a belief he brought into his own home, one which his wife, Betty, discussed in an interview after his assassination when she told the interviewer that Malcolm listened to her and they had an equal partnership.

The last belief of the Nation of Islam is that their god, Allah, already came to earth as a human being, and they believe that person to be Master W. Fard Muhammad. While they don't necessarily believe that Fard was Allah throughout his whole life, they do believe that the reason Fard started the Nation of Islam in July 1930 is because Allah entered his body to help Fard start the religious organization. They also add a little disclaimer under their twelve beliefs that states that, to the members of the Nation of Islam, Allah is God, and he is the only God. They note this because the members of the Nation of Islam tend to use the words "Allah" and "God" interchangeably throughout their written beliefs and scriptures.

A List of Demands From the Nation of Islam

In his book, Elijah Muhammad answered the ten most common questions that people ask about the Nation of Islam. The first answer is that the Nation of Islam wants complete freedom for African Americans. This is one of the most common statements that Malcolm discussed. The members of the Nation of Islam don't believe they will obtain this complete freedom until they move back to Africa.

The second answer Muhammad discusses is the most common question he receives from people is that along with freedom; they also want complete and equal justice under the law. There are several examples throughout this book about the unequal treatment African Americans face in the justice system. Nation of Islam members want justice for their race not only against the crimes committed against them but also for African American who are accused of crimes.

The third point Muhammad makes is that the Nation of Islam is fighting for equal opportunities in all areas of society. African Americans want the opportunity to be able to gain the best opportunities, the same ones which are available to other races of society.

The fourth point discusses the separation of races. During many of his speeches, Malcolm X discussed how he felt that white America and African Americans would never be able to live in the same area. In his book, Muhammad discusses more about this, giving an explanation as to why the Nation of Islam believes descendants of slaves should receive their own territory. Muhammad goes on to state that this territory could be part of United States soil, but Malcolm always stated that all African Americans should go back to Africa and establish their own civilization. When Muhammad gives the reasoning for why members of the Nation of Islam feel this way, it's because African Americans and white America have never been able to live together in harmony. This makes the Nation of Islam believe that the two races will never be able to live together in equality. Muhammad further discusses that because the slaves gave so much sweat and worked for the slave owners for free, the descendants of the slave owners should have to provide the territory for the descendants of the slaves. Not only should they provide the territory, but the descendants of slave owners should also have to supply the African Americans with anything they need in order to sustain life and property. Muhammad wrote that the descendants of slave owners should only need to supply everything for the next couple of decades because, after this amount of time, African Americans will be able to provide for themselves.

Part of the fifth point discusses how the Nation of Islam doesn't mean African American men and women should be forced to go live in other lands provided by the descendants of the slave masters. Muhammad discusses how this choice would be completely up to the descendants of the slaves. The other piece of the fifth point discusses how all the African Americans held in the prison system should regain their freedom, in both the north and the southern states. At the end of this point, Muhammad states that the Nation of Islam believes this is the best and only plan for whites and blacks to live conflict-free.

The sixth point discusses police brutality. The Nation of Islam believes that the federal government should step in and find a solution to the problem of mob and police attacks against African Americans. Muhammad further discusses that the government should make sure that African Americans receive justice when they are brutally beaten. Malcolm X discusses this in various speeches and messages throughout his time with the Nation of Islam. Muhammad further states that white Americans who break the laws and become unnecessarily violent against African Americans should be held accountable for their actions and be punished accordingly in a court of law.

In the next point, Muhammad goes back to when he discussed descendants of slave owners providing land and supplies to descendants of slave owners. He states that the Nation of Islam believes that if African Americans cannot receive these supplies and territory, then the United States should give them equal rights under the law and equal employment opportunities as soon as possible. The Nation of Islam's leader states that because they worked for hundreds of years as slaves, African Americans shouldn't have to continue to live in poverty and rundown communities. They should be treated equally and well-respected due to all the free labor their ancestors were forced to provide for hundreds of years.

The eighth point on Muhammad's list is that if the United States government can't provide the equality the Nation of Islam demands, then the government shouldn't tax African Americans.

The ninth point speaks of education for African American children. The Nation of Islam states that they want their children to be able to obtain the best education. They want African American children to have equal education opportunities to white American children, but they want to keep separate schools. They want boys to be taught in these separate schools up to the age of sixteen and girls up to the age of eighteen. The Nation of Islam also agrees that African American teachers should teach African American students. They also demand that African American girls be sent off to colleges. Along with this, Muhammad states that the Nation of Islam wants the United States government to provide all the textbooks, school buildings, school supplies, and college buildings without asking the parents of the children to chip in any amount of money to help pay for the school system. The Nation of Islam further believes that the teachers in their schools should be able to teach their students how they see fit but in the most decent and respectful way.

The last point that Muhammad makes in this list is that the Nation of Islam believes interracial marriage should be illegal because they want the Nation of Islam to remain pure.

Malcolm Adds the X

After his conversion to Islam, Malcolm not only started studying about the Nation of Islam but began preaching his studies of prayer to others. During this time, Malcolm also became opposed to the Korean War. Because the Nation of Islam didn't support war, this meant the Malcolm didn't support war either. During 1950, Malcolm wrote a letter to President Truman not only discussing his views on the war but also stating that he was a communist. Due to the fear of communism in the United States at the time, the FBI got involved and began looking into this man known as Malcolm Little.

It was around this time where Malcolm Little started to sign his name as Malcolm X. In Haley's book, *The Autobiography of Malcolm X*, Malcolm explains that adding the X to his name was very symbolic as it stood for the family name he would never learn as his ancestors took that name once they became slaves. In a sense, Malcolm used the X to replace his last name because "Little" was the name of the slave owners who bought his family. Another part of this is because the Nation of Islam discussed this topic and often used the letter X to replace slave names.

Throughout his last two years in prison, Malcolm continued to not only preach about the Nation of Islam to whoever would listen behind bars, but he also continued to write letters to Muhammad. The two promised to get together once Malcolm left the prison walls, which occurred in August 1952 when Malcolm X was granted parole.

Many people who have studied the life of Malcolm X believe there are at least two major reasons he converted to the Nation of Islam religion. One of these reasons was because his brother, Reginald, talked about the Nation of Islam and was a huge supporter of the Muslim faith. From the time he was a child, Malcolm was a family man at heart and believed family was the foundation of society. No matter what was thrown at his family, specifically between himself and his siblings, they remained as tight as they could throughout their lives. While Malcolm was close to all his siblings, he was especially close to Reginald. It didn't take a lot of convincing from Reginald for Malcolm to look into the Muslim faith and start reading about the Nation of Islam because Reginald supported it and told Malcolm that the Nation of Islam would help him stay on the right path and get out of prison.

The second reason was because of the basis of the Nation of Islam faith, which was not only equality for African Americans but that they were the superior race and couldn't live in harmony together with whites. Malcolm knew about the belief some African Americans had that white Americans and African Americans would never be able to live in one country together as equals because of their long past of conflict and hate towards each other. But when Malcolm was growing up, the number of African Americans who believed this was low. In fact, while they continued to deal with racism, they also believed that one day the races could mix and live in a peaceful world. But, because of some of his life experiences, Malcolm started to believe early in his life that African Americans and white Americans would never be equal.

The piece of Malcolm's life which really made him believe that the two races could never live happily side by side was his life with the Gohannas family. While Malcolm felt that the family originally treated him like family, he soon came to learn that they thought of him more as a mascot because he was different. He also started to analyze the way the Gohannas family talked to him and quickly noticed that they spoke to him like they believed he was stupid and would never be able to understand what they understood. For example, in Alex

Haley's book, *The Autobiography of Malcolm X*, Malcolm discusses the way they talked, such as always telling Malcolm that African Americans were just that way and always would be. Once Malcolm realized what the Gohannas family thought about the African American race, he changed his mind about white families and African American families living close together.

Chapter 5: The Start of Malcolm X and the Nation of Islam

After his release from prison in August 1952, Malcolm X continued to wander the streets preaching about the Nation of Islam and what they taught. This included, but was not limited to the white population being devils, the original people of this world being black people, and whites not being superior to blacks. The Nation of Islam also taught that the ending of the white population was bound to happen. All the teachings that Malcolm X and other Nation of Islam members preached were a mix of black nationalism and traditional Islam. While the National of Islam did promote racial unity, this was something that Malcolm X didn't believe in during this time as a Nation of Islam member, so it was something that he never really spoke about. Instead, Malcolm discussed more of the ways that African Americans needed to handle the white race and that there would never be complete freedom or equality for African Americans until they either left the United States and moved to where their ancestors came from, which was Africa, or, as the superior race, they started to take control of white people.

Birth of a New Nation of Islam Minister

Originally, Malcolm received a job working at the Ford Motor Company upon his release from prison. While he worked there, he started to realize that the Nation of Islam leader,

Muhammad, needed men to become ministers and help build the Nation of Islam. Malcolm quit his job and began working as a minister. In Alex Haley's *Autobiography of Malcolm X*, Malcolm states that it didn't take him long to realize he wanted to become a minister under Muhammad. Malcolm stated he always had activism in his sights, especially after his release from prison and becoming a member of the Nation of Islam. Furthermore, Malcolm felt that he could help all the brainwashed African Americans if he became a minister. From late childhood, Malcolm felt that most of the African Americans he knew were brainwashed in believing not only that white American citizens liked them and treated them as human beings but also that whites and blacks could live in one country in harmony.

Malcolm knew that he had a gift for public speaking and knew he could reach a large number of African Americans through preaching the word and teachings of the Nation of Islam. So, he contacted Elijah Muhammad and told him he was interested in becoming a minister of the faith and knew, without a doubt, he could not only help Muhammad build the Nation of Islam but also help the organization reach more members than Muhammad imagined. Muhammad felt Malcolm would be a great minister for the Nation of Islam and told him that training would occur in his home and under his guidance. Malcolm agreed and went to Muhammad's home to begin his training.

In *The Autobiography of Malcolm X*, Malcolm told Haley that he had never studied so hard for anything in his life as when he set his sights on becoming the best minister he could for the Nation of Islam. Malcolm goes on to describe the things that Muhammad taught him during their classes together. These topics included the true nature of women and men, the Quran, the Bible, the real meanings and reasons behind what the religious texts say, the policies and rules of the Nation of Islam and why they these rules and policies exist, administrative procedures of being a minister of a temple for the Nation of Islam, and the organization of the Nation of Islam.

Every day Malcolm took one of the classes, he went to bed in complete awe. He never realized that something could speak to him so clearly. He also didn't realize the passion he could hold for something, especially a religious organization. During these classes, Malcolm started to feel that he, too, was one of the African Americans who the white citizens of America had brainwashed. He started to feel that these classes were truly opening his eyes to the world around him, more than the readings and discussions about the Nation of Islam had while he was in prison.

The more and more Malcolm worked with the Nation of Islam leaders, the more Malcolm felt he truly had found not only a hero but someone he could believe in. Psychologically, Malcolm had found someone who, after growing up without a good male role model and so many years of feeling like a second-class citizen and sometimes not even like a human being, he could completely trust. And this was a huge step for Malcolm, because he didn't trust easily, and he didn't fully believe in the word of the Lord until he started reading about the Nation of Islam and Allah. For Malcolm, it was Allah who gave him the strength and the friendship he had so desperately wanted for so many years.

After Muhammad felt he had taught Malcolm X all he could about becoming a minister for the Nation of Islam, he sent Malcolm to Boston. In Boston, he worked with Nation of Islam member Lloyd X. Malcolm started preaching the words of the Nation of Islam inside the home of Lloyd X, who would further guide Malcolm.

Chapter 6: Malcolm X and the Nation of Islam

"Any time I have a religion that won't let me fight for my people, I say to hell with that religion. That's why I am a Muslim." — Malcolm X[7]

When Malcolm first started preaching the word of the Nation of Islam, he followed the way he was taught and the way he saw other ministers preach. Malcolm didn't change the teaching or his words too much, though he did enjoy starting with an analogy of his own creation.

While Lloyd X watched Malcolm preach, he started to realize that Malcolm had a special way with words and a very special public speaking talent. He sat back and watched the people in his living room listening to every word Malcolm stated. During his regular preaching sessions, Malcolm would not only talk about the white race as blue-eyed devils, but he also discussed how whites brought the African ancestors to America on slave ships. He discussed not only the cruelty the African ancestors had to face by the white slave owners but how this devil work from the white race began on the slave ships. Malcolm usually used the example of how white men started raping African women while they were chained down in a slave ship. Malcolm felt that this was a good topic to examine because it was one of the most publicized crimes between white American citizens

---

[7] Enisuoh, A. (n.d.). The Nation of Islam (Black Muslims) | Socialist Alternative. [online] Socialistalternative.org. Available at: https://www.socialistalternative.org/life-legacy-malcolm-x/nation-islam-black-muslims/.

and African American women.

When Malcolm spoke, he engaged the audience in a way that they felt not only included but pulled in by his words. People who heard Malcolm X speak often stated that even though you could be in a large crowd, you would feel like he was speaking to you and no one else in the room. On top of this, people felt that Malcolm would preach in a way that was not only convincing but also understanding. Malcolm wasn't one of the preachers who would quote a lot of scriptures or state biblical words that no one really understood. Plus, because Malcolm believed in what he was teaching so strongly, he spoke very passionately about the words of Allah and the teachings of the Nation of Islam. At the end of all his sessions, Malcolm would ask his audience to stand if they believed in what they had heard. Of course, nearly everyone Malcolm spoke to would stand up.

This sent chills down the spine of not only Lloyd X but also Nation of Islam leader Muhammad. Both knew they had found a gold piece for their religion in Malcolm X, and they knew that he would come in handy for various reasons within the religious organization. For Malcolm, he became happy because he finally felt he had found somewhere he truly belonged and which would allow him to help the African American population. While his teaching followed the strict code for the first few months, soon Malcolm was off and helping to establish temples for the Nation of Islam in the areas he knew and where people knew him. Once this started, Malcolm began to find his own way of preaching.

For Malcolm, it didn't always matter what the original teachings of the Nation of Islam were if he didn't agree with them. He simply noted, when he disagreed, that what he was saying wasn't his idea; it was Elijah Muhammad's. Malcolm did this by starting what he was about to say with "The Honorable Elijah Muhammad teaches us..."[8] And because Malcolm X was such a great speaker, who quickly proved he could make thousands upon thousands of people listen to him in one sitting, he was compelling. However, there was always a piece of the original belief in what Malcolm X was preaching.

Other Nation of Islam members noted after a few years that Malcolm X often did the opposite that Elijah Muhammad would ask of him. For instance, when Muhammad told his ministers they weren't to get into politics or to discuss politics in their sermons, Malcolm started to get interested in politics. The members who realized this didn't understand why Malcolm would do this and when they questioned him about it, he would usually shut them down in various ways. Some of the members of the Nation of Islam started to believe that Malcolm didn't realize he was doing it, but others felt he knew exactly what he was doing, and this made them nervous. For some of the Nation of Islam members, Malcolm became too powerful too quickly while Muhammad lived somewhere else and paid very little attention to how Malcolm preached because, to the leader of the Nation of Islam, Malcolm kept bringing up the membership numbers and that was what mattered to Muhammad.

Slavery Was A Prophecy in the Bible

[8] Teachingamericanhistory.org. (n.d.). A Summing Up: Louis Lomax interviews Malcolm X | Teaching American History. [online] Available at: http://teachingamericanhistory.org/library/document/a-summing-up-louis-lomax-interviews-malcolm-x/.

One of the teaching from the Nation of Islam is that the majority of African Americans, if not all, are descendants of slaves. These slaves came to America through the Atlantic slave trade, which was when they were no longer allowed to gain any sort of education. Not only did slaves have to stop learning, but they weren't allowed to teach their children any type of knowledge. This didn't just include the basics of math, reading, and writing, but it also including learning their own religion, culture, language, and history. Once American men captured Africans in their own homeland, they lost all their rights, including the right to learn. Because of this history about their ancestors, the Nation of Islam members believe that they have fulfilled one the Bible's prophecy of slavery. Because the Nation of Islam members' ancestors were slaves and fulfilled this prophecy, the members believed this made them closer to Allah and purer in the eyes of the Lord.

It didn't take long for Malcolm to start to believe this part of the Nation of Islam's teachings. In fact, Malcolm had learned something similar as a child due to his parents' respect and loyalty to Marcus Garvey and his beliefs. Garvey felt that the African race were universal masters before slavery and they would once again be superior to all other races. Malcolm quickly latched onto the belief that African Americans were the superior race because so many of their ancestors had been held in chains for hundreds of years.

Nation of Islam Beliefs on Race

Growing up feeling as though you were a second-class citizen was normal for African Americans during the era in which Malcolm lived. This thought, which was often something people generally believed as true, was psychologically damaging to anyone, and Malcolm became included in this category. From the time he was a child, Malcolm wanted to live in a world where he not only felt like he mattered to everyone but where he could feel safe on a daily basis. Unfortunately, this world never came for Malcolm; however, as he read about the teachings of the Nation of Islam, he came to believe that they were right on track, which was another reason he joined the faith in the early 1950s.

Today, it's well known that humans started to migrate from Africa. When Malcolm lived, this knowledge was out there, but many people, especially white Americans, didn't want to believe or preach it. Because of this, it wasn't discussed in schools and you rarely, if ever, found it in a textbook. So, when Malcolm read that the Nation of Islam taught this, he became overjoyed and immediately started to become more interested in the beliefs and words the members of the Nation of Islam spoke.

Not only did many Nation of Islam ministers, such as Louis X Farrakhan, discuss the belief that all races came from the African race, but Elijah Muhammad also wrote about it in his book, *A Message to the Blackman in America*. In his book, Muhammad states that it doesn't matter what color of skin a person has; they came from the black man. He explains that the reason skin color changed was because of a special method which Africans used as a form of birth control. He further explains that a man by the name of Yakub invented this type of birth control and created a plan where the new races, such as the white race, would come together and divide up the original race, which is the African race. Once the new race successfully divided the original race, the new race could take control over the original race through a series of lies and manipulation. They would then be able to control the original race for at least six thousand years. During this time, as they would pit one member of the original race against the other, they would then turn around and work to bring unity back into their lives.

While Malcolm listened to every word the Nation of Islam leader said, and every word he read about the religious organization, Malcolm still took what he learned and added a few his own beliefs. For example, not all members of the Nation of Islam taught that the African American race was superior to the white race. While Malcolm X wasn't the only member of the religious organization to preach this, he didn't fully get the idea from Elijah Muhammad. In fact, Muhammad could be accepting of white Americans, especially the ones who accepted or joined the Nation of Islam faith or who were of the Muslim faith. Muhammad also stated that their founder, Fard, had a mother who many believed was a white Muslim.

While Malcolm respected and adored Elijah Muhammad, he taught others that the white Americans who understood and respected African Americans knew that they were inferior to the black race. They didn't need to be taught or explained this.

Why Malcolm X and the Civil Rights Movement Didn't Mix at First

There were many differences between the Nation of Islam and the civil rights movement, and one of these was that as a Nation of Islam leader, Malcolm X told African Americans that they needed to gain their equality, at all cost, which included causing violence. This not only surprised the white population but also several African Americans because, prior to Malcolm X's words, they had heard civil rights leaders, such as Martin

Luther King Jr. speak about civil rights. Martin Luther King Jr. spoke the opposite of Malcolm X and not because he wasn't a Nation of Islam member; it was because King truly felt that peace between the white race and African American race could be fulfilled, but only through peaceful protests. For those who followed Martin Luther King Jr., no matter what occurred during their protests, including police brutality against them, they were never to retaliate with violence. Of course, the protests didn't always end with Martin Luther King Jr.'s followers listening to his every word, especially once Malcolm X and his National of Islam came into the mix. However, this difference also didn't mean that Malcolm X didn't focus his attention on the civil rights movement. He just did so in a way where he always mixed the Nation of Islam with the civil rights movement.

Another difference between what Malcolm X preached as a Nation of Islam leader during the civil rights movement and what Martin Luther King Jr. preached was the issue of voting. One of the biggest issues during the civil rights era was equal voting for the African American race. While Martin Luther King, Jr. and many other civil rights leaders began protesting at voting booths and going into the voting centers where they tried to register to vote, Malcolm X and other Nation of Islam leaders told their followers not to vote.

Malcolm X not only attacked some of the things the civil rights movement stood for but he also verbally attacked one of the movement's main leaders, Martin Luther King Jr. In his attacks, Malcolm called Dr. King several names, such as a chump. Malcolm continued to attack the civil rights movement, and some of Martin Luther King Jr.'s followers by stating that the protests they conducted, such as the famous 1963 March on Washington, were a waste of time. Malcolm X cited that he felt either brainwashed African Americans or whites ran the organization and he didn't understand why groups became excited about marching in front of a statue of a president who didn't like them when he was living.

For many people, these differences caused more problems than what the civil rights movement previously had. While some people looked at it in complete amazement because two of the major civil rights leaders were telling their groups to do two different things, other people, especially of the white population, started to wonder why they should become one with the African American race when the people of the African American race couldn't even treat each other with equality.

On the other side of the coin, some civil rights movement followers of Martin Luther King Jr. either left his group completely to join the Nation of Islam, or they started bringing violence into the protests. For the people who did begin to follow more of the way Malcolm X and the Nation of Islam preached, they later cited their reasoning as being tired of having to wait for justice and freedom, which was what they felt many of the leaders of the civil rights movement were doing. Instead, they wanted action, and action was exactly what Malcolm X and the Nation of Islam preached.

Chapter 7: Malcolm Helps the Nation of Islam Grow

While he started preaching during his time in prison, Malcolm continued following in his father's footsteps once he gained his freedom in August 1952. One of the first things he did was travel to Chicago, so he could meet the leader of the Nation of Islam, Elijah Muhammad, who he still conversed with through letters. Through their meeting, Muhammad talked about starting temples in other areas of the United States, such as Boston, New York, and Philadelphia. Malcolm liked this idea and because he knew the places well, volunteered to help Muhammad in any way he could. Muhammad took Malcolm up on offer and soon, new Nation of Islam temples were finding their way close to where Malcolm lived.

However, Malcolm didn't stop his practice of Islam with the work of new temples. In the basement of his home, Malcolm started to publish the newspaper of the Nation of Islam, which came to be called *Muhammad Speaks*. On top of this, Malcolm started a process to get the newspapers out on the streets. Because they weren't selling well at first, Malcolm decided that every male who was a member of the Nation of Islam should be given a number of copies to hand out in the streets in their communities. Through this, Malcolm further created a fundraising technique which allowed the Nation of Islam to not only continue to grow their religious movement but which also helped spread the word on what the Nation of Islam stood for.

Along with publishing *Muhammad Speaks*, Malcolm took it

upon himself to make sure other African Americans in the United States understood how evil the white population really was towards their race. A lot of Malcolm's push to bring out this information happened because of Malcolm's memories from his childhood and young adult life. Malcolm analyzed every single relationship he had with a white person while he was in prison and came to the conclusion that the Nation of Islam was correct in stating all whites were evil. But Malcolm further remembered his prior analysis while walking around different African American communities and realizing that they were all brainwashed. Once Malcolm found the Nation of Islam, he started to blame the African American brainwashing on the white population. He believed that if the white population wasn't so untrustworthy, African Americans wouldn't be so brainwashed. Malcolm hoped that he would be able to wake African Americans from their brainwashed lives. They would then realize that the Nation of Islam was correct in stating that all white people were evil and that, in order to gain total freedom from the white population, African Americans needed to move back to Africa.

During this time, Malcolm held dozens of speaking engagements from standing on the streets in Harlem, New York City, and other areas, to speaking at colleges, such as the University of Oxford and Harvard University. People would quickly go to hear Malcolm speak not only due to his amazing power of speech but also because of his charming personality, intelligence, and wit. For many people, they had never heard anyone like Malcolm speak before, not just the way he spoke but what he spoke about. Instead of talking about how African Americans and whites could all live in harmony if they just put their hate aside and showed compassion towards each other, Malcolm spoke of the built-up anger African Americans felt towards the white race for the centuries of oppression they caused.

Once the Nation of Islam temples No. 11, in Boston, and No. 7, in Harlem, were completed, Malcolm began focusing his time within the walls of these temples. Here, he continued to spread the word of the Nation of Islam. Because of Malcolm's natural ability to speak and preach, the Nation of Islam Temple No. 7 quickly became one of the most prestigious Nations of Islam temples, right behind the headquarters, which was located in Chicago.

As the temples and the Nation of Islam organization grew, Elijah Muhammad quickly realized the talent that Malcolm X held in spreading the word of the Nation of Islam. Because of this, Muhammad started to hold a certain soft spot for Malcolm and began to bring him around to other areas within the Nation of Islam organization, such as giving Malcolm the title of National Representative of the Nation of Islam, which made Malcolm second-in-command, right under Muhammad.

Because of Malcolm's fast-growing interest in the Nation of Islam and how quickly the religious movement started to grow, from the building of temples to the number of members, the FBI started looking into Malcolm's actions. Just like a few years prior, the FBI worried about Malcolm's interest in communism. So, in 1953, they reopened the case of Malcolm and his possible involvement in communism.

In 1955, Malcolm continued to help build the Nation of Islam by founding more temples, such as Temple No. 13, located in Springfield, Massachusetts; Temple No. 14, which was built in Hartford, Connecticut; and Temple No. 15, which made its home in Atlanta, Georgia. With the help of these new temples, the membership of the Nation of Islam religious movement grew at an astounding rate every month. In fact, in an average month, the Nation of Islam received hundreds of new memberships.

With Malcolm as second-in-command under the Nation of Islam, membership quickly started to grow, along with Malcolm's popularity. It's believed that at its height, the Nation of Islam could claim as many as 500,000 members, all of which were members during Malcolm's time with the Nation of Islam.

Chapter 8: Malcolm the Family Man

Just a couple years after his release from prison and starting his career as a minister under the Nation of Islam, Malcolm married a woman by the name of Betty Sanders. She met Malcolm during one of his ministry lectures about the Nation of Islam in 1955. Falling in love not only with Malcolm's charismatic personality but also his strong passion for the Nation of Islam and great public speaking skills, Sanders soon started going to as many as Malcolm's lectures as she could attend. Around a year later, in 1956, Sanders officially converted and became a member of the Nation of Islam. After becoming a member, Sanders officially changed her name from Betty Sanders to Betty X.

Like a few other religions, the Nation of Islam looked down on one-on-one dates. Therefore, when the couple started seeing each other, they kept to courting and stuck with crowded events, such as dances and lectures Malcolm gave on the Nation of Islam. In order to make sure that Betty understood he was serious for her, Malcolm would make sure to invite her to his lectures in New York, where he would speak in the libraries and museums around the city.

Malcolm X finally proposed to Betty X on January 12, 1958, while they were on the phone with each other. At the time, Malcolm was in Detroit, and the couple decided to not wait much longer as, two days later, on January 14, 1958, the couple had their wedding day.

Their marriage was to follow the marriage laws set forth by the Nation of Islam, which meant that Betty X was to follow her husband's rules. However, over the course of their marriage,

Betty started to change her tune with how their marriage worked. While she continued to listen and obey Malcolm's demands, he started to become more and more demanding and, after a few years, Betty could no longer handle all the demands, and she spoke up about marriage equality.

For Malcolm, someone who had grown increasingly angry over the course of his life over the inequality he and other African Americans faced, the words Betty spoke to him hit home and he began to think about her words. A few years after Malcolm's death, Betty discussed their marriage and that moment. She stated that one night after Malcolm gave her a list of demands he wanted to see in his wife, she turned around and gave him a list of demands she wanted to see in her husband. But, instead of getting angry, Betty stated that Malcolm looked at her and said, "Boy, Betty, something you said hit me like a ton of bricks. Here I've been going along, having our little workshops, with me doing all the talking and you doing all the listening."[9] From that moment on, the marriage dynamic between Malcolm and Betty X changed as their marriage not only became more equal, but Betty gained more independence.

During their decade of marriage, which lasted until Malcolm X was murdered, the couple had a total of six children. Their first daughter, Attallah, came into this world during the same year her parents got married, 1958. Two years later, Qubilah entered their lives, and she was followed by the couple's third daughter, Ilyasah, who was born in 1962. Gamilah Lumumba, the couple's fourth daughter, followed the line of girls in 1964. Then, after the death of their father, the couple's twin daughters, Malikah and Malaak, came into the world.

---

[9] Watch The Yard. (n.d.). Did You Know That Malcolm X's Wife Dr. Betty Shabazz Was A Member Of Delta Sigma Theta?. [online] Available at: https://www.watchtheyard.com/deltas/malcolm-x-wife-betty-shabazz-delta-sigma-theta/.

One of the most intimate ways people can learn about the real Malcolm X is through his daughter, Ilyasha Shabazz's, book, titled, *Growing Up X: A Memoir by the Daughter of Malcolm X*. While Ilyasha has no memory of her father's assassination, which she witnessed with her little two-year-old eyes, she wrote a telling book about the memories of her father as passed down from the people who knew him best. The book was originally started by Malcolm's wife, Betty, because she wanted the world to get to know the Malcolm she knew. The first time Betty wrote about her husband was in a 1969 essay titled "Malcolm X as a Husband and a Father." This essay surprised people all over the world as they never imagined the man who became known as the most twisted and angriest man in the United States could be so gentle, kind, and loving.

Betty discussed how Malcolm would often work while his family enjoyed the beach. She talked about how he would write his speeches while he watched her and the children build sand castles and play in the water. She also talked about how he strove to give his daughters the best education they could receive, and this started at home as he would often read stories and poetry to them. She also talked about how Malcolm would often compliment her in his own way, such as saying he could cook but never did because he felt she was such an amazing cook.

Betty made the point that family life was the center of Malcolm's life; no matter how much he worked or traveled, he made sure to keep his family first. When he traveled, he would often schedule days so he could go see his family as often as possible, providing they couldn't travel with him at that time. Betty also stated that people could have easily picked up on how family life was center in Malcolm's life through his speeches, but most people focused more on the negative things he said. For instance, in a 1963 speech, Malcolm discussed the

African American communities and his observations on the sad state of African American families. In this speech, given at the University of California, Malcolm stated that were too many African American babies who came into this world without a father for various reasons. He discussed how the African American communities not only needed to band together to help raise these babies but also needed to find a solution so young African American girls stopped giving birth at such a young age and before they found a husband to help them care for their families. Instead, Malcolm continued, too many African American girls were giving birth as teenagers and were unable to find husbands because men don't often want to marry a young woman with a baby.

Of course, Betty's essay, which became the basis for her daughter's book, made Malcolm X's critics come to the table for another feast. Instead of seeing the point Betty was trying to make, that Malcolm X centered his speeches on the family unit because he believed the family was the foundation of society, they started to state that such soft stories couldn't save Malcolm's reputation. Malcolm's critics continued to state that no matter what his family tried to say about how kind and gentle he was, to the American population, he remained the violent, twisted man he always was.

But Malcolm's wife and daughter are not the only family member who have tried to show the world the real Malcolm X. Another family member who wrote a book which details some of the life of Malcolm X, another piece of him the public never understood, was Rodnell Collins. Rodnell, daughter to Malcolm's half-sister Ella, whom he lived with during his teenage years and into his early twenties, wrote a book titled *Seventh Child*. This book discusses the important role Ella played in Malcolm's life and how much he looked up to her. Through the book, Rodnell details the valuable role family played in Malcolm's life and why he felt family was so important. For instance, Rodnell discusses Malcolm's criminal life, which turned into becoming a minister for the religious organization Nation of Islam, and then his transformation during his pilgrimage to Mecca, supported by one of Malcolm's biggest fans, Ella. Not only did she continue to support Malcolm as he was running around the streets of New York and Harlem breaking the law, drinking, and gambling, but she helped fund his journey to Mecca as she knew this was something he needed to do. Not only because he wanted to complete the journey as a Muslim, but because she felt it would help him find himself and help him grow into the person he wanted and needed to become.

Chapter 9: Malcolm's Rise Into the Spotlight

While Malcolm X started to make a splash in the world before 1957, his focus was mainly on the building of the Nation of Islam and not so much the civil rights movement. However, that was always a part of Malcolm's message too. But Malcolm had a different version of civil rights, which would change throughout the rest of his life. Malcolm would discuss how African Americans and white people could never live together in harmony as African Americans would never gain their complete freedom from the chains the white American population held. It would be the things Malcolm taught while he was a member of the Nation of Islam which would send him soaring into the spotlight.

For many people, seeing an African American come out with a different view of civil rights and not support the civil rights movement brought out people's curiosity. From there, they would start looking at Malcolm X as that "strange one." Malcolm welcomed the lens of the camera as it meant he could reach more African Americans.

Malcolm X obtained even more attention when he befriended a man named Cassius Clay, more commonly known as Muhammad Ali. Through their conversations, Malcolm reached Ali enough that he decided to convert to the Nation of Islam. While Malcolm and Ali eventually had a falling out, this conversation made people realize how powerful Malcolm could be with his words and the passion he had for the Nation of Islam. To some, this realization was refreshing, especially to members of the Nation of Islam and its leader. But to others, this realization became very scary, especially for members of the police department, because they soon realized how much power Malcolm had over people. None of them believed this was a good thing.

The Hate that Hate Produced

Another move Malcolm made which landed him a role in front of the camera lens was a documentary he became a part of in 1959. The documentary, *The Hate that Hate Produced*, focused on African American nationalism and showed on WNTA-TV in the New York and New Jersey areas. This documentary was a five-part series produced by Louis Lomax and Mike Wallace. The documentary focused on the Nation of Islam, a group which Lomax had become interested in as an African American but not necessarily as anything he wanted to join. Lomax, along with two white camera operators, were given a backstage pass into the Nation of Islam's temples and faith. Not only did Lomax gain access to interview some of the Nation of Islam's biggest ministers, such as Malcolm, but he also gained access to some events within the Nation of Islam's religious organization.

The creators of this documentary contacted Malcolm X and asked him if he, along with others from the Nation of Islam, would be interested in filming a documentary about their religious organization. Of course, Malcolm told Lomax that he couldn't say yes or no because the only one that could was the leader of the Nation of Islam, the Honorable Elijah Muhammad. Lomax then booked a flight to Chicago where he met up with Muhammad. According to Haley's book, *An*

Autobiography of Malcolm X, Muhammad had several questions, concerns, and perhaps a few demands before he allowed cameras into the Nation of Islam.

Malcolm stated that once they started filming for the documentary, they not only spoke with several members of the Nation of Islam, such as himself and Elijah Muhammad, but they also took audio and video recordings of their messages during services.

It was through this documentary that people not only got a rare glimpse into the Nation of Islam, but they also learned of the University of Islam, also known as the Muhammad University of Islam, at the time, a school for children who were members of the Nation of Islam. This school, established in 1934 by Nation of Islam leader, Elijah Muhammad, taught children to hate the white race. Of course, their curriculum also held the basic classes of math, science, history, and taught them about civilization.

Learning about this school was very shocking to the majority of non-Nation of Islam supporters, including other civil rights leaders. But that wasn't the only shocking part of the documentary for people who weren't part of or didn't understand the religious organization. This documentary opened the eyes of many white families who didn't know that there was such a religion or that it was so hateful towards the white race. It also opened their eyes to see that there was a different side to the civil rights movement, a more radical side.

African Americans had mixed views on the documentary, and their views often depended upon where they lived. Most African Americans in the northern states dealt with racism, but nothing like the southern states, so they didn't feel that there was such a need for so much anger towards the white race. While they wanted equality like all other African

Americans in the United States, most northern African Americans felt there was a better way to go about it. The further south in the United States you went, the more African Americans agreed with the harsh words in the documentary. But there were still a few southern African Americans who felt that there wasn't a need for that much hostility towards any race.

For Malcolm X, the documentary made him a household name. Prior to the release of *The Hate that Hate Produced*, Malcolm wasn't seen much in mainstream media. While many people knew who Malcolm X was, most of them knew of him because he lived around them, had heard him speak as a minister of the Nation of Islam, or were members of the religious organization.

This documentary wasn't the only publication that the Nation of Islam had within that year. At the same time they were filming the documentary, a professor from Boston University, C. Eric Lincoln, spent time learning about the Nation of Islam. Through his research, he worked to create a book about the religious organization. With this book coming out around the same time as the documentary, people really started to notice the Nation of Islam, with many becoming more curious as to what this religious organization was really about.

The documentary and the book also helped the Nation of Islam organization grow. Within a week of its television premiere, the membership of the religious organization grew from around 30,000 to over 60,000. Of course, this number wasn't only an amazing number for the ministers of the Nation of Islam but also for the organization's leader, Elijah Muhammad, who only dreamed of one day receiving a membership so high. But this wasn't even the strongest point of the growth in membership for the Nation of Islam. In fact, not too long after this, the Nation of Islam hit its top peak in the number of members within the organization. It's recorded that the most the organization reached was 125,000 members.

Many researchers who study the life of Malcolm X believe that one of the biggest reasons the membership for the Nation of Islam grew to such a high number so quickly was because of Malcolm X. He had an amazing talent for public speaking, one that could easily draw a person in and make them believe nearly everything he stated. But he also had a personality which would make people become interested in him and want to know more about what he preached due to the fact that they were interested in the person known as Malcolm X.

Malcolm himself didn't particularly care why people were listening to him or wanting to know more about the Nation of Islam. He just wanted people to learn about the religious organization, so he could teach them what it really meant to be an African in the United States. Malcolm realized that no matter why or how people started listening to his speeches and messages, he could reach them and bring them into the religion or at least make them begin to critically think about what type of relationship the white race truly had over the African race. For Malcolm, their interest due to the documentary and the book just made it easier for him to get what he considered the truth out to African Americans. And for Malcolm, at the time, this truth basically stated that African Americans were the superior race and that they needed to move back to Africa to gain their complete freedom, among many other teachings of the Nation of Islam. Of course, sometimes, Malcolm would twist the Nation of Islam's teachings into his own version, which sometimes caused issues between other members of the Nation of Islam.

Malcolm's Surprise from the White Race

In Haley's book, *The Autobiography of Malcolm X*, Malcolm discusses one of the most interesting things that happened after the documentary and book came out. Malcolm stated that after the media release, he started to receive hundreds of letters daily, but most of them were from the white race and not African Americans. Malcolm explained that, surprisingly, very few of these letters were death threats or any type of negative criticism. In fact, they were from white people who felt that he was right and they feared what God was going to do when he came back to earth and saw the world in which they were living.

Malcolm further stated that many white people agreed with Elijah Muhammad's teachings. However, they didn't fully agree with the Nation of Islam believing African Americans had to move back to Africa to gain full freedom. They also didn't usually agree with calling them devils as they supported the Nation of Islam, its members, and its leader, Muhammad, and should not be grouped with white people who didn't support African Americans and the Nation of Islam.

Malcolm took these letters to heart and immediately started to work on changing his speeches up a bit to explain what he and other members from the nation of Islam meant when they stated that white Americans were blue-eyed devils. Malcolm explained in his speeches that when they said this, they were not talking about every single white person. Instead, they were talking about the history of white Americans as a whole; the history of their cruelties towards the African and African American race. The members of the Nation of Islam were talking about white Americans' history of the greed and evils they had bestowed upon the African American race for centuries because they felt they were superior to them and therefore treated African Americans as the devil would treat someone.

Malcolm would then go on to explain that the white Americans who understood that their ancestors did the African American race wrong in history were not classified as devils. Instead, those members of the white race were intelligent and honest people who understood that the harm that their ancestors caused with the Atlantic slave trade still damaged the descendants of the African American slaves.

Hinton Johnson Event

One of the first reasons Malcolm X became a household name across the United States was the Hinton Johnson incident. This event occurred on April 26, 1957, when Johnson, a member of the Nation of Islam, and a couple of other members noticed police officers brutally beating an African American male with nightsticks. In an attempt to help their fellow African American, they ran to the policemen while yelling at them that they were in New York and not in Alabama.

Unfortunately, this only made one of the policemen turn on Johnson, who was severely beaten by the New York City police officer. Then men were then arrested and taken to the police station. A witness to the beatings got in contact with Malcolm X and told him what had happened to Hinton Johnson. In response, Malcolm X called up a few more of his Nation of

Islam brothers and, together, they went down to the police station, where they demanded to speak to Johnson. At first, the police told them they hadn't booked anyone who was part of the Nation of Islam. However, after a crowd of nearly five hundred Nation of Islam members grew outside of the police station, they allowed Malcolm to see Johnson. Upon seeing Johnson, Malcolm demanded that they call an ambulance to take him to the hospital.

While doctors treated Johnson at the hospital, they learned that he had subdural hemorrhaging and brain contusions. Johnson was treated at the hospital and then released and sent back to the police station where he would remain under arrest. By the time Johnson returned to the station, a crowd of nearly five thousand people had gathered outside of the police station, where they not only supported Johnson and the Nation of Islam but also demanded answers as to what Johnson did to deserve such awful treatment.

When Johnson returned, Malcolm X and his lawyer were working on bail money to release a couple of members of the Nation of Islam, but they were unable to pay the bail for Hinton Johnson, as police told them he couldn't leave until he was arraigned the next day, and this included Johnson being unable to go back to the hospital. At this point, Malcolm X realized that there was nothing more they could do, so he went outside and told the crowd to leave by giving a hand signal.

The police who saw Malcolm give the hand signal and watched the crowd disperse became very alarmed at how much power Malcolm X had over the members of the Nation of Islam. They quickly realized that so much power shouldn't be given to one man and started a surveillance program on Malcolm X. However, it wasn't only the police department in the city of New York that had their sights on Malcolm X; they continued to contact other police stations where Malcolm lived and had gone to prison, such as Harlem. After discussing the situation of Malcolm's power over the members of the Nation of Islam, the police departments all agreed to keep Malcolm X under close surveillance.

While the case went to trial, the grand jury didn't indict the officer who beat Hinton Johnson so badly; he caused him to have a subdural hemorrhage, which is a collection of blood between the skull and the brain. This only made Malcolm X grow angrier not just over the treatment of African Americans and the unequal justice system, but also over the treatment of the members of the Nation of Islam. In response to the trial, Malcolm X wrote the police commissioner an angry letter, letting him know what he thought of the situation and of them. Of course, this letter only furthered the police department's efforts on surveilling Malcolm X.

More Malcolm in the Late 1950s

Malcolm X continued to find the spotlight not only with the Nation of Islam but also with the civil rights movement in the late 1950s. It was during this time that Malcolm X, who started to refer to himself as Malcolm X Shabazz or Malcolm Shabazz, became a more prominent figure on the television screen.

The modern-day civil rights movement skyrocketed into the mainstream spotlight in December 1955. While the movement started several years before this time, it was Rosa Parks, a civil rights activist, who brought media attention towards the movement. On December 1, 1955, Rosa Parks was heading home from a long day working as a seamstress at a retail store when the Montgomery city bus she was on started to become overcrowded. Soon, the bus driver noticed that white passengers were unable to find seating. Because the Montgomery city buses were segregated, usually with the first four rows designated for whites and the rest of the bus for African Americans, the bus driver removed the "colored only" sign towards the back of the bus. This meant that the African Americans sitting in the first few rows of the original "colored only" section needed to move further towards the back of the bus. Everyone complied with the bus driver's request except for Rosa Parks, who would not move. The bus driver threatened to call the authorities, and Rosa told him to do so. That night and into the next day, Rosa's arrest made headline news all over the United States. Four days later, on December 5, one of the largest and most successful boycotts during the modern-day civil rights movement took place with the start of the Montgomery Bus Boycott. Rosa Parks is credited with starting the movement.

With the civil rights movement now in the spotlight, and Malcolm's views often different from most other views, he found this to be one of the best times to start spreading the word of the Nation of Islam. While he befriended some civil rights leaders, such as Rosa Parks, many others had mixed feelings about Malcolm X due to his hostility towards the white race. However, this often worked in his favor as Malcolm brought out the emotions that many African Americans were trying to keep hidden.

Once Malcolm started expressing his thoughts on violence within the civil rights world, more and more people began to understand what he was talking about. Simply stated, Malcolm X felt that if people were violent towards African Americans, they had every right to be violent back. There was no denying that thousands of people, especially members of white supremacist groups, such as the Ku Klux Klan and the Black Legion, became extremely violent towards all African Americans, including children, which really outraged Malcolm. This made Malcolm feel that the only way to begin to gain their freedom, to gain the promises they had received during the creation of the United States, was to act like them. While other civil rights leaders, such as Martin Luther King Jr., disagreed, many activists, such as Rosa Parks, understood Malcolm's point of view.

Malcolm discussed his point of stating that African Americans should retaliate with violence when they were attacked with violence. In Haley's book, *The Autobiography of Malcolm X*, Malcolm states that the biggest reason people, especially white Americans, became overly critical and dramatic over his saying that violence was okay for African Americans was because he was an African American male who condoned violence against white Americans. During Malcolm's time, this was something that people didn't do or discuss. They would often use the excuse that white people acted so violently against African Americans because those beliefs had been put in their heads. All African Americans needed to do was continue to have patience and, one day, whites would no longer accept violence against African Americans.

But when it came to violence against African Americans, especially when they were just trying to defend themselves against attacks, patience wasn't something that Malcolm X believed in. Malcolm X believed in the old rule of an eye for an eye. If someone is violent to you, then you can defend yourself with violence, and this is acceptable because it's known as self-defense.

Malcolm further discussed how the thought of allowing one group to be violent towards another group and then not allowing this group to retaliate against the violence wasn't a Christian way of thinking. During Malcolm's lifetime, religion was an important piece of the American lifestyle. People often stated that the reason they could or couldn't do something was that it was or wasn't Christlike. Malcolm believed that there wasn't anything Christlike when it came to allowing white American men to brutalize African Americans because of the color of their skin. Of course, many of Malcolm's critics were angered when they heard about Malcolm's take on violence as a response to violence. But this didn't bother Malcolm; to Malcolm it just meant that they knew he was right and just didn't want to admit it.

Malcolm continued to receive the spotlight into the 1960s, especially among other African leaders. In 1960, when the United Nations General Assembly met in New York, they invited Malcolm to various meetings and events which focused on Africa. He met leaders such as Kenneth Kaunda of the Zambian African National Congress, Ahmed Sekou Toure from Guinea, and Gamal Abdel Nasser of Egypt. During the United Nations General Assembly, Malcolm X also met with Cuba's Fidel Castro, who invited him to Cuba for a visit because he became so impressed with his take on topics and the way he spoke.

Chapter 10: Departure from the Nation of Islam

During the early 1960s, Malcolm's relationship with Nation of Islam leader Elijah Muhammad started to drift. Malcolm, who had spent over a decade building up the Nation of Islam religious organization, soon started to see a change within the Nation of Islam and his good friend Muhammad. Malcolm's biographers, along with historians who have studied Malcolm's life, state that there were three major steps which caused Malcolm to drift away from the Nation of Islam leader and eventually decide to leave the organization.

Part of Malcolm's reasoning behind his leaving the Nation of Islam were his ever-changing personal views. While Malcolm believed everything the Nation of Islam leader, Muhammad, and other members of the religious group taught him at first, soon, he began to change some of his views. On top of this, members of the Nation of Islam also started to change their views as the organization itself began to change internally. Much of this had to do with all the change going on in the United States, but some had to do with the fact that Malcolm X was constantly evolving as an individual and educating himself with various topics. Over time, with what he read and analyzed, along with his life experiences and finding guidance in other people he began to look up to, Malcolm X slowly started to back away from the Nation of Islam but didn't realize it immediately.

Muhammad Doesn't Support Malcolm's Decision

One of the first steps that started to destroy Malcolm's relationship with Muhammad began during the latter part of 1961. During this time, the Los Angeles Police Department and members of the Nation of Islam started to have violent confrontations between each other. One of the bigger riots between the LAPD and the Nation of Islam happened on April 27, 1962, when police met with several Nation of Islam members and, when the confrontation started, the police began to beat the members.

Several other Nation of Islam members quickly realized what was going on and ran outside to help their friends. Once the officers realized more Nation of Islam members were coming out of Temple No. 27, they realized there were too many members and called for backup. Within minutes, around seventy police officers from the department came and started to assist their colleagues. While the riots resumed outside, with Nation of Islam members getting beaten and shot while other members continued to try to disarm the officers, other officers went into Temple No. 27. Inside, they randomly started to beat Nation of Islam members.

By the end of the night, at least seven Nation of Islam members had been shot by police. One of those members was Korean War Veteran Ronald X Stokes, who witnesses stated was raising his hands to surrender when an officer shot him in the back. The bullet later killed him. Another member was William X Rogers, who officers shot in the back. While Rogers lived, the bullet paralyzed him. After the incident, several Nation of Islam members were arrested, but no charges were going to be filed against any of the police because the coroner ruled that Roland Stokes' killing was justifiable.

Upon hearing the news of what had happened at Temple No. 27, Malcolm X became irate. Following through with his belief that any amount of violence against African Americans should result in violence, he quickly got ahold of the toughest and most violent Nation of Islam members he could find. Malcolm's plan to take action against the police for their violence against African Americans started, but because the group was about to take this on as Nation of Islam members, they needed to seek approval from Elijah Muhammad. Surprisingly, to Malcolm, Muhammad refused to approve the plan or Malcolm's request to take action against the police.

As Malcolm X considered another option because Muhammad had denied his first plan, he started to notice a change in not only Muhammad but many Nation of Islam members. First, he started to notice that several Nation of Islam members were starting to befriend civil rights movement members, which was something Muhammad had refused to allow his followers to do earlier. On top of this, Malcolm also noticed that members were not only supporting local African American politicians, but they were starting to work for them in various capacities.

After Malcolm's assassination, several members of the Nation of Islam were questioned about why Malcolm had left the Nation of Islam organization. When asked, Nation of Islam member Louis X, who was one of Malcolm's close friends, stated that Muhammad's refusing Malcolm's request to attack the police was the biggest turning point.

A Different Side to Elijah Muhammad

Around the time of the Temple No. 27 incident, rumors started going around about Nation of Islam leader Elijah Muhammad's extramarital affairs with the secretaries for the Nation of Islam. At first, Malcolm refused to believe these rumors and figured they were started by an angry former Nation of Islam member of a random person who wanted to try to get rid of the Nation of Islam. Malcolm couldn't believe that Muhammad would go so far as to break one of the most important teachings of the Nation of Islam.

But, over time, Malcolm started to hear about more women accusing Muhammad. To try to get to the bottom of the situation, Malcolm first contacted Muhammad and asked if the rumors were true. Muhammad told Malcolm that those actions were against the policies of the Nation of Islam and he would never do such a thing. But Malcolm still didn't feel right about the situation, so he decided to do a little more digging. Malcolm found out who some of the accusers were and contacted them. They all told Malcolm what had happened, which made him start to believe that Muhammad had committed the acts. Next, Malcolm got ahold of Muhammad's son, Wallace, and spoke to him about the rumors. After this, Malcolm came to the conclusion that Muhammad had more than likely had the affairs. However, he didn't want to accuse him without confirmation.

Malcolm received his confirmation from Muhammad in 1963. Not only did Muhammad admit to having extramarital affairs with several secretaries of the Nation of Islam, some who didn't even come forward to accuse him, but he tried to justify his behavior by using biblical prophets. While Malcolm couldn't stand the actions of Muhammad, he continued to remain a Nation of Islam member and preacher. But he also continued to back away from the religion, feeling that he couldn't fully believe in what he had to preach anymore because of Muhammad's actions.

Kennedy's Assassination, the Nation of Islam, and Malcolm X

The third step which caused a breaking point between Malcolm X, the Nation of Islam, and its leader, Elijah Muhammad, had to do with the Kennedy assassination. Most citizens of the United States were shocked and saddened over the murder of the thirty-fifth president, John F. Kennedy, on November 22, 1963. Because Kennedy was a big supporter of the civil rights movement, people wanted to know what Malcolm X thought because, while he supported civil rights, he didn't support the civil rights movement.

Immediately after Kennedy's assassination, Nation of Islam leader Elijah Muhammad told his members that they were not to speak about the assassination, especially to the press. Instead, the Nation of Islam organization sent public condolences to the Kennedy family. But, when the media asked Malcolm X for his comment about the assassination, he called the situation "chickens coming home to roost."[10] The phrase meant that people who had done bad things in the past would have bad things happen to them in the future. Malcolm further stated that when this type of stuff happened, he didn't get sad over it. Instead, he felt happy because the person

---

[10] Nytimes.com. (n.d.). MALCOLM X SCORES U.S. AND KENNEDY; Likens Slaying to 'Chickens Coming Home to Roost' Newspapers Chided. [online] Available at: https://www.nytimes.com/1963/12/02/archives/malcolm-x-scores-us-and-kennedy-likens-slaying-to-chickens-coming.htm.

deserved it. Not too long after Malcolm's comments about Kennedy's assassination, he continued to make comparisons to other horrible events which had happened earlier, such as the bombing of the Birmingham church where a few African American girls died and other assassinations of civil rights leaders.

The remarks by Malcolm X made the public, including many members of the Nation of Islam and the civil rights movement, angry. In response, Nation of Islam leader Muhammad told Malcolm that he could not speak publicly for three months. However, he could continue to hold his place as minister of the Nation of Islam. Of course, this didn't sit too well with Malcolm as not only did he believe in rights and equality for African Americans, but he also believed in the right of public speech. This drove the final wedge between Malcolm X and Muhammad, along with most of the members of the Nation of Islam.

While Malcolm would wait a few months before announcing his departure from the Nation of Islam, he continued to cause friction between himself and the religious organization. By now, even with his latest statements against the tragedies that had taken the American media by the storm, such as the assassination of President Kennedy, Malcolm remained popular in the spotlight. The news of Malcolm X working on an autobiography caused further outrage for members of the Nation of Islam, including Muhammad. On top of this, people were taking Malcolm's speeches and starting to create them into books. Many Nation of Islam members began to see Malcolm as a bigger threat to Elijah Muhammad and the religious organization than a friend.

Malcolm's Split from the Nation of Islam

Malcolm X publicly announced his departure from the Nation of Islam organization on March 8, 1964. He stated that, while he had kept his religious beliefs as a Muslim, he would no longer be a part of the Nation of Islam as he felt their beliefs weren't where they were supposed to be and he could no longer preach or believe in what they did. He further stated that he was in the process of creating his own African American religious organization, which would create a better belief system for every African American Muslim. He stated that his organization would bring out the political consciousness of African Americans.

During his announcement, Malcolm further stated that he wanted to start working with other civil rights movement leaders. He told the crowd that, before, he had been unable to do so, and had had to keep away from the civil rights movement because those were the orders he received from Elijah Muhammad.

Of course, this announcement further angered not only the members of the Nation of Islam but Elijah Muhammad himself. The person the religious organization felt they could trust and respect had turned on them in a public setting. From then on, while the Nation of Islam did whatever they could to keep their plans quiet, dozens of members began to plan assassination attempts and send death threats not only to Malcolm X but also to his family. In response, Malcolm started to travel with bodyguards wherever he went.

Chapter 11: Life After the Nation of Islam

After the public realized Malcolm had left the Nation of Islam, members of the Sunni faith spoke and wrote to Malcolm about their religion and encouraged him to become a member. Like with anything Malcolm did, he not only discussed the faith with its members but also did his own studying on the religion. It was during this time that he changed his name again as he started to call himself El-Hajj Malik El-Shabazz, which fit more into the Sunni religion. However, to the rest of the world, he would always be remembered as Malcolm X.

Change of Views

Malcolm X always seemed to be thinking, and this didn't change once he left the Nation of Islam. In fact, after his departure from the religion, his views started to become more independent, which was something he always felt all African Americans should do as he believed other people had brainwashed too many of them.

During his time as a member of the Nation of Islam, Malcolm X spoke a lot about the views of Marcus Garvey, his father, and the views he had read in the Nation of Islam about separating religions. He was one of the first civil rights leaders to tell African Americans that they would never fully gain independence in America, due to not being able to live equally with the white population, and that all African Americans should move back to Africa. Malcolm preached that in Africa, they would find pure freedom. However, once he left the Nation of Islam and started to become more involved with other leaders of the civil rights movement, his views changed. He soon started telling people that if African Americans became strong in black nationalism and independence, they would be able to attain full freedom while living on American soil and living next to other races.

Closer towards the end of his life, Malcolm started to realize that his previous views about the white race weren't completely true. He stopped believing that they were the devils and started to see that thousands of white people wanted to help the black race just as much as anyone else. For Malcolm, it was his travels after leaving the Nation of Islam that opened his eyes to realize that people of all races could help each other.

Malcolm also started to realize that while he complained about everyone else being brainwashed by society, he, too, had been brainwashed while a member of the Nation of Islam. A few days before his death, Malcolm X talked about how he now realized there was a sickness inside of him which held him in chains, making him believe certain things he thought he truly believed in but didn't. He then went on to state that he was happy to be released from those negative thoughts and this helped give him a taste of freedom.

During the last year of his life, Malcolm X began working alongside a lot of other civil rights leaders he had wanted little to do with as a Nation of Islam member. One of these leaders was Martin Luther King Jr., whom he met on March 26, 1964, as they both attended the debate about civil rights at the Senate hearing. While Malcolm began working with other civil rights organizations and leaders, he became open about what policies he felt they needed to change. One of the biggest points Malcolm made was how people considered the civil rights movement a struggle. Instead, Malcolm stated that it should be less of a struggle and more of a human rights issue. Malcolm also realized that in order to become the strong civil rights leader he wanted to become, he needed to separate politics and religion. So, while he continued to work on his religious organization, he did his best to keep the politics out of his religion and the religion out of his work with the civil rights movement.

Malcolm X also stated that calling the movement a struggle kept the movement on United States' soil, and really, it was a human rights issue for people all over the world. When discussing his beliefs on this further, Malcolm X made the point that if it became more of a national issue, they would be able to get together with other nations and take the issue in front of the United Nations. Malcolm believed that the United Nations would give them, and everyone else who supported the issue, more support than what they would ever receive in the United States, especially during their lifetimes. Malcolm X focused on what his actions would do for the future generations. By this time, Malcolm was a father and, like so many other civil rights leaders, he wanted to create a better life for his children, and for every other African American child.

Malcolm X also began to preach that instead of trying to focus on gaining protection from the white population, especially authorities, African Americans should start to protect themselves. In order to work to create equality in a world where they had been given so little for so long, they needed to start to treat their own race with respect and compassion in order to gain the same from other races. Malcolm X told African Americans that in order to make sure they attained equality, justice, and freedom, they needed to defend each other by whatever means necessary.

Malcolm's Organizations

After Malcolm left the Nation of Islam, he wanted to focus his attention on the areas of African American life he wanted to help build and change, especially the areas he couldn't previously address as a minister in the religious organization. Malcolm had learned a lot over the years, not only with his role as minister under the Nation of Islam but also through listening to other African Americans and observing the world around him. Through his observations, Malcolm also learned that African American education had to be taught in the school systems. While some schools, mostly African American schools and a few segregated ones, focused on African history, Malcolm felt that what the schools taught, their textbooks, and how the schools taught the information could use a lot of improvement. Therefore, with the help of friends, other civil rights advocates, and former members of the Nation of Islam, Malcolm came up with a plan to build up African American education with a focus on African history, culture, and roots.

Muslim Mosque, Inc.

Malcolm X founded the Muslim Mosque, Inc. religious organization in March 1964, which he announced less than a week after leaving the Nation of Islam. The organization would only last about a year, as it ended when the life of its leader ended. But throughout that year, the small religious group gained a membership of over fifty people, with most of them former members from the Nation of Islam. The majority of those members left when Malcolm X announced his departure from the Nation of Islam.

While the organization only lasted for a short year, Malcolm X did amazing things for the members of the organization during that year. While he communicated mainly through letters as he mostly traveled out of the United States during 1964, he continued to help the organization grow. He also sent them letters explaining his newfound beliefs, especially about how the white race weren't devils and how many were working to help the black race. Of course, this received mixed reviews from the members of the Muslim Mosque, but it didn't stop people from joining. In fact, within a couple of months after its establishment, over one hundred people had joined the organization.

The Muslim Mosque, Inc. organization started to hit the mainstream not only when members who weren't previous Nation of Islam members began to join, but also when twenty members received scholarships. In late summer of 1964, the Supreme Council on Islamic Affairs handed out almost two dozen scholarships so young members of the Muslim Mosque could attend Al-Azhar University without having to worry about paying their tuition.

Organization of Afro-American Unity

Malcolm, along with John Henrik Clarke, Gloria Richardson, Jesse Gray, and other black nationalists formed the Organization of Afro-American Unity (OAAU) on June 24, 1964. Malcolm wanted to establish a group that brought African unity, culture, and history to African Americans.

Similar to the Organization of African Unity (OAU), a group which created a unified voice for Africans by bringing together over fifty nations, Malcolm wanted to focus on the over twenty million African Americans to promote independence and unity. This organization focused on four basic principles: education, economic security, reorientation, and restoration.

For education, the organization focused on changing African and African American history within the school systems. Malcolm and the other founders knew how poorly their race's history was written in the textbooks, and the organization vowed to find ways to change this. One of the ways would be to have African Americans create their own textbooks about their history. They would further educate the children, so they could learn the values that the organization stood for, such as promoting economic independence and unifying the black race with other nations.

Restoration focused on re-establishing communication with Africa. They wanted to help African American officially release themselves from the bondage their ancestors faced while being held as slaves on American soil. The principle of reorientation became one of the most basic principles of the organization. They wanted African Americans to educate themselves with the history of Africa and its culture through reading educational books.

Economic security focused on not only becoming more financially independent as individuals but also on becoming financially independent from each other, including other Africans around the world. Malcolm knew that one of the reasons the white population had established the Jim Crow laws and other segregation and restrictive laws after the end of slavery happened was because the whites were afraid of African Americans. They feared African Americans gaining an education because they worried about them being able to take over America. While Malcolm didn't directly promote taking over the American government, he wanted African Americans represented in the government, and he wanted to create a special bank. This bank would not only secure funds for African Americans and their community but also make them a source for other African nations who struggled economically.

Journey to Mecca

Malcolm's pilgrimage to Mecca would become one of the biggest turning points near the end of his life. Every Muslim sees a visit to Mecca as a holy obligation, providing they can make the trip. While Malcolm couldn't financially support himself on the trip, he was able to secure a few funds from his older sister, Ella.

Unfortunately, Malcolm's journey to Mecca didn't start as well as it ended. Because he wasn't able to speak Arabic and was a United States citizen, authorities questioned if Malcolm was a Muslim or not, so they held him until he could gain proof. After receiving the book *The Eternal Message of Muhammad*, written by Abdul Rahman Hassan Azzam, Malcolm tried to contact the author. While he wasn't able to reach the author, he got in contact with the author's son. After hearing about his situation, Azzam not only helped get Malcolm released but allowed Malcolm to stay in his hotel room. Following his release, Prince Faisal designated Malcolm as a state guest. Once Malcolm completed the pilgrimage and Hajj rituals, he met with Prince Faisal and, to his surprise, a unified Muslim audience.

In a famous letter, Malcolm spoke of his amazement of how unified and equal the crowd was, "Never have I witnessed such sincere hospitality and overwhelming spirit of true brotherhood as is practiced by people of all colors and races."[11] Because of this, Malcolm realized that people could become united because he saw members of the audience of different races and skin color treating each other with respect and equality. He saw a large group of people from all over the world and different cultures who believed in the same religion, focusing on the same rituals and celebrating together after its completion. For the rest of his life, Malcolm often discussed how shocked and amazed he became over this sight and he felt the crowd truly made him believe that people could overcome racial inequality. In the letter, Malcolm went on to discuss how he believed that the main way the United States would end its racial segregation and issues was by learning and understanding the Muslim faith. Of course, once the letter reached Malcolm's friends and family, they had trouble believing such a sight. Some members from the Muslim Mosque, Inc., couldn't believe what they were reading and thought Malcolm was either lying or that something else had happened.

Malcolm's pilgrimage to Mecca did more for him than just show him that the white race and black race could come together as one. In Haley's book, *The Autobiography of Malcolm X*, Malcolm discusses all the realizations he made while he stayed in the hotel room in Mecca, along with many other Muslims who were on the same journey. Not only does Malcolm talk about the flashbacks he has to his childhood,

---

[11] X, M. (2018). Malcolm X: The Pilgrimage to Makkah - IslamiCity. [online] Islamicity.org. Available at: https://www.islamicity.org/6279/malcolm-x-the-pilgrimage-to-makkah/.

memories he thought were gone forever, but he also talks about his life as a Nation of Islam member.

This is also the only time Malcolm takes to really discuss what he really felt and thought about Muhammad during his Nation of Islam days. Malcolm states in *The Autobiography of Malcolm X* that he truly believed Elijah Muhammad had no human faults. He not only respected and believed in him as a human being but also as something beyond a human, like a true holy believer, who couldn't do anything wrong. Malcolm believed that it wasn't possible for Muhammad to make a mistake. At that moment, Malcolm realized how dangerous it is for any human to hold another human on such a high pedestal. He further stated that believing a human is divine isn't mentally healthy because it isn't possible for any human to not make mistakes. It also causes more issues when the person realizes that this divine human being does make mistakes and isn't as pure as the person believed.

Malcolm's trip to Mecca made him realize many things about his past, including previous beliefs, that led him to realize he didn't always have the best beliefs for any human. At that moment, Malcolm realized that it didn't matter who was fighting to better society and humanity as a whole. It didn't matter if the person was African American, Mexican, white, or Canadian. What mattered was that a person wanted a better and more equal life for his fellow Americans and would work to help make that better life a reality for everyone.

When Malcolm discusses his trip to Mecca and the aftermath in Haley's book, *The Autobiography of Malcolm X*, Malcolm talks about how the media circuits in the United States didn't want to discuss the differences in his beliefs. They didn't want to talk to him about how he went on his pilgrimage to Mecca and discovered a better path for humanity in their fight to create a more equal world for African Americans. Instead, they wanted to focus on how Malcolm liked to stir the pot when it came to African Americans and the civil rights movement. They wanted to continue to discuss the beliefs and thoughts Malcolm had before his pilgrimage because that Malcolm brought in more ratings and was more interesting than the Malcolm who returned from his journey to Mecca.

Malcolm Continues his Travels

Throughout the last year of Malcolm's life, in 1964, he focused more on traveling than staying in the United States. One of the reasons for all his travels was because he knew in order to unify the African nations, and people from African descent all over the world, he needed to meet national leaders. Another reason was because Malcolm was so amazed by his trip to Mecca that further traveling became his calling. He believed it would help continue his work at home by opening his eyes to different cultures, people, and experiences. Many people feel Malcolm planned to continue his travels after he returned to the United States in 1965.

Africa

While Malcolm had previously visited the African continent, he returned in 1964, immediately after his pilgrimage to Mecca. He didn't stay long, as he had plans to return to the United States, but promised to make another return soon. He kept his promise as he left Africa in May and returned the following month.

By this time, Malcolm had become a celebrity in many parts of the world, including Africa. Once he stepped foot in Africa, Malcolm became busy giving interviews for television and radio stations in various places, including Nigeria, Guinea, Algeria, Morocco, Egypt, Liberia, Nigeria, and Ethiopia. Not only did he meet with nearly all of Africa's main leaders, but he also attended a meeting of the Organization of African Unity as a representative of his group, the Organization of Afro-American Unity. By the end of his trip, Malcolm had not only received inventions to join governments from Egypt, Ghana, and Algeria but had also received the honorary name "Omowale," which means "the son who has come home." To Malcolm, this was a treasured honor.

Malcolm's Return to the United States

Before returning to the United States in the fall of 1964, Malcolm decided to make a couple stops. First, on November 23, he stopped in Paris, France, where he gave a speech at the Salle de la Mutualite. A week later, he made a stop in the United Kingdom so that he could get in on the Oxford Union Society debate. A couple of months later, Malcolm made a stop in London so that he could give a speech in front of the Council of African Organizations.

Once Malcolm returned to the United States, he continued his speaking engagements in various locations, such as Alabama. He not only spoke in front of community crowds, but he also started to speak regularly at universities. As he traveled, he kept his work with the MMI and OAAU close with him as his organizations were always the focus of his speeches.

People became further interested in getting Malcolm to speak in interviews, for documentaries, or in various books authors were writing. Not too long before his assassination, Malcolm met up with Robert Penn Warren, who published his book *Who Speaks for the Negro?* in 1965. When the book discussed the topic of segregation in the Nation of Islam, Warren sought an interview with Malcolm, who agreed to give him information.

Chapter 12: Murder of an Icon

On February 21, 1965, Malcolm X was at the OAAU in Manhattan's Audubon Theater and Ballroom, getting ready to give a speech. A couple of days prior, he had told reporters he knew members of the Nation of Islam were trying to kill him. Since Malcolm left the religious organization, he had received dozens of death threats.

A year before Malcolm's assassination, the Nation of Islam repeatedly threatened Malcolm in several ways. For instance, in February 1964, Temple No. 7's leader ordered her members to bomb Malcolm X's car while other members told each other that Malcolm deserved to be killed. In December 1964, Louis X, who was a close friend of Malcolm's when he was a Nation of Islam member, wrote in *Muhammad Speaks* that Malcolm X was worthy of death. The events continued into 1965 when members of the Nation of Islam set Malcolm's house on fire. Even though Malcolm brought his bodyguards with him for extra protection, no one would be able to save him from what was about to happen.

With about four hundred people in the audience, Malcolm and his bodyguards heard a disturbance. They started to try to quiet the audience when a man ran up near Malcolm and shot him. The majority of witnesses claimed that all they could remember were gunshots and yelling. When the chaos ended, and the investigation began, investigators found out that the first man who shot Malcolm used a sawed-off shotgun and hit him in the chest. After his shot, two other men ran towards Malcolm with semi-automatic guns and started shooting. First responders came and rushed Malcolm to Columbia Presbyterian Hospital, but doctors couldn't do anything to save him. They pronounced Malcolm dead at 3:30 in the afternoon.

With so many witnesses, including Malcolm's bodyguards and members of his family, authorities quickly reached the suspects, especially the first person to run up and shoot Malcolm as several members of the crowd caught him and beat him before the cops came. All three of the suspects were members of the Nation of Islam. Talmadge Hayer, also known as Thomas Hagen, was the first shooter and the one beaten by members of the audience. While he admitted to shooting Malcolm, he claimed the other two suspects, Thomas 15x Johnson and Normal 3X Butler, were innocent.

The autopsy report revealed they shot Malcolm twenty-one times in several areas of his body, including his chest, legs, arms, and left shoulder. While Hayer continued to state Johnson and Butler were innocent, all three men were convicted on murder charges and sentenced to life in prison, but none of them would remain in prison. In 1985, Butler received his parole. Johnson was paroled in 1987 and continued to protest his innocence until his death in 2009. Hayer received his release from prison when he was paroled in 2010.

Nearly thirty thousand people came to say their goodbyes to Malcolm X through his public viewing, which the family held between February 23-26. Malcolm's funeral, which was held at the Church of God in Christ Temple, occurred on February 27. Not only did the family provide loudspeakers so the crowd could hear the services outside of the temple, but the service also played on live television.

Actor and activist Ossie Davis gave the eulogy, stating that the reason Malcolm didn't worry about death was because he was not only willing to die for what he believed in but to die for the people who believed in him. Dozens of other civil rights leaders attended Malcolm's funeral, including Bayard Rustin, James Farmer, Andrew Young, John Lewis, Jessie Gray, and James Foreman.

A group of Malcolm's friends took it upon themselves to become his gravediggers. Malcolm made his forever home in Hartsdale, New York, at the Ferncliff Cemetery. After the death of Malcolm, several civil rights activists, friends of Malcolm X, and other celebrities gave money to the Committee of Concerned Mothers charity. Established by Juanita Poitier and Ruby Dee, this charity focused on not only raising funds to provide a new home for Malcolm's family but also created a savings account so his children would receive a good education.

Reactions to the Death of a Controversial Civil Rights Advocate

Because the public either loved or hated Malcolm X, the reactions people had to his death were mixed. One of the most famous reactions is a telegram which was sent by Martin Luther King Jr. In this telegram Dr. King sent to Malcolm's wife, Betty, he told her how saddened and shocked he was to hear of Malcolm's assassination. He went on to tell Betty that he always had a soft spot for Malcolm because of his passion to help build the African American communities up through economic stability, education, and not only understanding of African history but also understanding of their roots. He further told Betty that he admired how Malcolm could find the root of the issue through direct observation, intelligence, and educating himself. Even though Malcolm and Dr. King didn't see eye to eye, not even after they started fighting in the civil rights movement together, Dr. King felt Malcolm held some of the strongest passion out of all the civil rights activists to change the problems African Americans faced in their daily lives. Dr. King also stated that he thought Malcolm had a very eloquent way of speaking and said no one could deny the talents he gave this world.

Martin Luther King Jr. further went on to give his thoughts on not only Malcolm X's assassination but also on Malcolm X. He wrote to the *New York Amsterdam News,* where he noted that Malcolm's views of hatred and violence stemmed from growing up in a time where there were no civil rights movements to try to change Malcolm's life. And the life he lived as a child would only create a person such as Malcolm X because he had no one to help teach him that violence wasn't the answer until he came to the conclusion himself, but too close to the end of his life. Dr. King continued to discuss how Malcolm had changed over the years and was growing into a greater leader than anyone could have imagined. Dr. King stated that he respected Malcolm's leadership skills because it was these skills that helped bring about the focus of the civil rights movement and that change needed to happen in the African American communities because they were not second-class citizens but equal to white American citizens.

On the other side of the coin, when asked how he felt about his one-time close friend and minister of the Nation of Islam, the religious organization's leader stated that Malcolm got what he deserved as what ended his life was exactly what he had preached about for years. Of course, Muhammad spoke about Malcolm's death during the time when members of the Nation of Islam were being held for his assassination. When Muhammad discussed this part, he stated that the Nation of Islam never wanted to murder Malcolm as they knew they wouldn't have to because his own life, choices, beliefs, and statements would lead him to his own death.

The news media also extensively discussed Malcolm's death, not always positively. For instance, the *New York Times* wrote that Malcolm X wasted his life as he turned things which were peaceful into a world of violence. They continued to state that while Malcolm X held many talents, he used them for the purpose of evil and was a twisted individual. But the *New York Post* gave a different statement on the death of Malcolm X when they stated that even his toughest critics couldn't deny the intelligence and talents Malcolm X possessed in his lifetime, especially with public speaking and his willingness to go to immeasurable lengths to create the life that African Americans had not only been promised but had only dreamed of coming true. They also stated that it was unfortunate that no one would be able to learn the great places Malcolm X could have taken the African American community.

It wasn't just˙American citizens and news reporters that provided positive or negative thoughts about the assassination of Malcolm X. One of the biggest areas of support Malcolm X had received in life came from Africa, and this didn't change after his death. While several leaders and citizens of Africa gave their condolences to his family, friends, and the United States, the press was especially sympathetic to the loss of a great leader and friend. For example, the *Ghanaian Times* stated that Malcolm X was among the most extraordinary leaders of the world to ever step foot in Africa. They compared him to the likes of Medgar Evers, Patrice Lumumba, John Brown, and many others who people of African descent regarded as some of the greatest leaders in their history. The *Guangming Daily* in China stated that the only reason Malcolm X died was because he was brave enough to fight for the freedom and equality of his people.

Conspiracy Theories

Not everyone felt that the Nation of Islam were to blame for Malcolm X's death. Other civil rights leaders, such as the head of the Congress of Racial Equality organization, James Farmer, believed drug dealers were the true murders. Other civil rights advocates turned to the lack of police protection for Malcolm X, especially after he had received so many death threats prior to his assassination. They blamed the authorities, such as the FBI, CIA, and the New York Police Department. Not only did people blame the authorities because they failed to protect an American citizen, but because investigators failed to secure the crime scene.

In fact, witnesses noticed the police officers didn't seem a bit concerned about the situation that had just occurred. They stated that when the policemen entered the ballroom where the assassination took place, none of them had their guns out or were worried about being shot at. Of course, this only increased the conspiracy theory that the authorities had something to do with the death of Malcolm X.

Then, a few years after the death of Malcolm X, people learned about an FBI program known as Cointelpro, established by the authorities to cause problems within civil rights groups. After more information about Cointelpro came out, more and more people started to believe that the FBI definitely could have been involved in Malcolm's assassination. Before Malcolm died, he told a reporter that one Nation of Islam member, John Ali, was an undercover agent for the FBI. The conspiracy theory grew when people learned that John Ali and the man who admitted to killing Malcolm X, Talmadge Hayer, met the night before Hayer murdered Malcolm. On top of this,

Malcolm stated on more than one occasion that his biggest rival was John Ali.

Malcolm's wife and children believe that Louis Farrakhan, also known as Louis X, was one of the people responsible for Malcolm's death. Later in his life, Louis dropped hints on more than one occasion, including an interview with the television show *60 Minutes*, that statements he made might have led to the assassination of Malcolm. However, Louis also stated that he never ordered Malcolm's assassination.

While three members of the Nation of Islam were tried and convicted of the murder of Malcolm, no one really knows who actually killed him or ordered his assassination. While people continue to look into his death, including circulating petitions asking the government to release his files, nothing has been done or released.

Chapter 13: How Malcolm's Reputation Changed

While part of the world was devastated over Malcolm's assassination, the other part of the world felt they had just been saved from one of the most hateful and twisted men in the United States. While Malcolm had a few life-changing moments in the last few months of his life, many American citizens didn't realize this. Other American citizens didn't care that he started to become a more caring and understanding person of all races, because they felt that people don't change, and Malcolm X was still inside of the more caring Malcolm.

Some people started to change their views once Alex Haley's book, *The Autobiography of Malcolm X,* hit stores just a few months after Malcolm's murder. Most of the people who read the book started to believe that he was just another lost soul in the world who was trying to make his own way in life. Others started to understand Malcolm and how Malcolm Little became Malcolm X. Some started to see his transformation throughout life as amazing, while others saw parts of it as alarming. But, no matter what a person's thoughts were on Haley's book, no one could deny the praise the book received. While Haley, Malcolm, and the book had their share of critics, people really felt that they could get to know the real Malcolm X through this book because of his honest nature.

But for several years, many people couldn't forget the man who called himself the angriest man in the United States. They couldn't forget how he called all white citizens the devils and how he pushed violence into the civil rights era when the civil rights movement tried to do nothing but bring out silent or nonviolent demonstrations. Other people couldn't forget that he was once an atheist criminal who spent time in prison before he became a popular minister of the Nation of Islam. They also couldn't forget that he tried to preach how African Americans were superior to the white race.

It wasn't just the stereotypical white conservative who had a problem with Malcolm X and wasn't fazed by his assassination; there were thousands of liberals who felt the same way. For them, the civil rights movement was a way for African Americans and the whites to get together and try to create a more equal and positive world for the African Americans. Most liberals believed that if they could create this world, it wouldn't just create a better world for the African American children, but it would create a better world for all children.

Over the course of the last couple decades, Malcolm X's reputation has greatly changed from people remembering Malcolm as the violent civil rights activist who stated he was the angriest African American to a more understood historical figure who just wanted to create a better world for his race but struggled with finding his own identity.

Through reading Alex Haley's *The Autobiography of Malcolm X*, people can get a good understanding of Malcolm's struggle for identity and the need to feel like a human being just like everyone else. When people not only started to read but also started to analyze *The Autobiography of Malcolm X*, views started to change on the civil rights leader. Not only did they start to see him as someone who was just trying to create a better life for African Americans, but they started to see Malcolm as a human being, which was one of the things he wanted out of life.

Another reason Malcolm X's reputation has changed from the angriest man in the United States to a legend of the civil rights era is because people's views on not only the Nation of Islam but also Muslims, changed during the 1980s and 1990s. People stopped seeing Muslims as second-class citizens and started viewing them more as next-door neighbors. On top of this, people's views about the African American race in general began to change, as they continue to change today.

Malcolm lived in a time where many white people, especially in the southern states, grew up believing that African Americans were different from them because that was what they were taught to believe. From a young age, many children during the early to mid-1900s were told that African Americans weren't like the white race. Some parents stuck with the age-old tradition of explaining to their children that African Americans weren't as smart, so they wouldn't be able to accomplish the same things, and they lived their lives differently. When this view started to change inside of people, Malcolm X's reputation also started to change. In a nutshell, some people didn't give Malcolm X a good reputation because he was an African American.

Another reason Malcolm X's reputation started to change was because people began to focus on the more positive pieces of Malcolm's life than the negative. For instance, instead of focusing on the hatred Malcolm X spread between African Americans and the white population, people started to focus on the educational opportunities Malcolm began to establish near the end of his life.

Once people started focusing on the later life of Malcolm and analyzing the change within his belief system, they started to wonder what type of leader Malcolm would have become if he had lived. Many people feel that he would have been able to create a better world between the African Americans and white population due to his eye-opening experiences when he made his pilgrimage to Mecca. Others feel Malcolm would have created a better world not only for African Americans but also for Muslims, as near the end of his life, he started focusing on creating more equal and better relationships among Muslims. Malcolm began to realize that he couldn't change relationships between everyone at once, but he could start with one section at a time. And because Malcolm came to believe that one of the best ways to achieve harmony, understanding, and compassion among one another was through the Muslim faith, he started there.

Many other people feel that Malcolm would have created better educational opportunities for African Americans. He would have helped African American children understand where they came from and guided them to find their roots to their home country. This would have helped African Americans begin to create their own sense of identity in a world where they are still often pushed to the side due to the color of their skin. Not only would he have helped children find their roots, but he would also help have educated them with African culture and history through better textbooks.

Other people believe that our country would be farther along in many different areas of life, not just equality between African Americans and white people. People believe Malcolm had the wisdom and talent to help fill the equality gaps between races, religions, and genders. Overall, thousands of people in the United States believe that if Malcolm had survived, he would have continued to help create a better and more equal country.

Malcolm X was a great leader, and the positive changes he could have made in a divided world were only beginning when he was gunned down that fateful February day in 1965. The reality is, no one knows what Malcolm could have done if he had survived. We can only continue to imagine and wonder what such a great mind, with a new change of passion and heart, could have done for a divided country.

Chapter 14: Malcolm's Legacy Continues Today

Malcolm X's legacy goes way beyond building the Nation of Islam and his civil rights work. There is no denying, no matter how you feel about his original stance on violence, that Malcolm X was one of the most influential African Americans of the twentieth century. Through his push for African Americans to realize that they came from somewhere before their ancestors were brought over on slave ships and given a different last name, African Americans began to look into their heritage. They also started to gain more self-esteem as they started to realize that they could become whatever they wanted to become, no matter what other people thought or said. Due to Malcolm's message from his teacher in high school, who told him he couldn't become an attorney because he was African American, Malcolm made sure to get across to other African Americans that they could dream and follow those dreams.

For many African Americans, Malcolm X made them realize the truth of how they were feeling due to years of oppression from white Americans. Several believed that Malcolm X was more real in the ways the world worked against African Americans than other civil rights leaders, such as Martin Luther King Jr. They also believed Malcolm when he stated that if African Americans weren't given the freedom they were promised with the founding of the United States, one day, they would take over, and white America would have to pay.

Malcolm X is often credited for bring out the black pride movements, such as the Black Arts Movement, the Block Power Movement, and the slogan "Black is Beautiful." After Alex Haley released Malcolm X's autobiography, *The Autobiography of Malcolm X,* more people began to realize how influential Malcolm X was during the civil rights movement. As people learned about his childhood, drug life, prison, and then realized what he became after his release from prison, they started to see how much influence his story could have on the younger generation. Not only is Malcolm X's life story one of struggle and hardship, but it's one about overcoming those issues and facing them while standing up for what you truly believe in. And not just standing up for yourself, but standing up for everyone around you, whether they believe in you or not.

Those who knew Malcolm X best know that he would do anything for any African American, whether they liked him or not. He wasn't afraid of death because, as Malcolm said himself, "If you're not ready to die for it, put the word freedom out of your vocabulary."[12] Malcolm X not only fought and died for the freedom of every African American in the United States but for all future generations as well.

Films and Books

Starting about a decade after his assassination, Malcolm X became a popular historic figure to portray both on Broadway

---

[12] Goalcast. (n.d.). 20 Malcolm X Quotes to Inspire You to Take Control of Your Life. [online] Available at: https://www.goalcast.com/2018/10/03/malcolm-x-quotes/.

and on the big screen. One of the most successful movies about Malcolm is the film *Malcolm X*, released in 1992, with Denzel Washington playing the famous historic civil rights icon. Martin Scorsese directed the film, which become one of the best films of the 1990s.

The release of *Malcolm X, The Greatest* came in 1977, and in 1981, a made-for-television movie titled *Death of a Prophet,* starring Morgan Freeman, became popular. Actors have also portrayed Malcolm in several movies detailing the times of his life, specifically during the civil rights era. These movies and television shows include *Betty & Coretta,* released in 2013, *King of the World,* and *Ali: An American Hero*, both released in 2000. Nigel Thatch also portrayed Malcolm X in the famous 2014 film, *Selma.*

Dozens of books for people of all ages have been written about Malcolm X. For adults, some of these books include George Breitman's *Malcolm X Speaks: Selected Speeches and Statements*, published in 1965 along with Alex Haley's *The Autobiography of Malcolm X*. Other than Malcolm's autobiography, there is no other written work by him. So everything people want to learn that came directly from Malcolm must come from the speeches he gave throughout the civil rights years. The majority of these speeches have made their way into several books.

Besides George Breitman's book detailing a few of Malcolm's speeches, others include *The End of White World Supremacy: Four Speeches by Malcolm X* (1971) and *Two Speeches by Malcolm X*, which was released in 1965. Other popular books which include speeches given by Malcolm X are *The Speeches of Malcolm X at Harvard* (1968); *By Any Means Necessary: Speeches, Interviews, and a Letter by Malcolm X* (1970); and *February 1965: The Final Speech* (1992).

Malcolm Little: The Boy Who Grew Up to Become Malcolm X, which was published in 2014, is one of the greatest books for the younger generation who wants to learn about Malcolm X's life. Malcolm's daughter, Ilyasah Shabazz, is the author of the book, which talks about how Malcolm grew up to become Malcolm X through the help of his big and loving family. The book, which was created to be an inspirational book for children to aim for their dreams and stand up for what they believe in, discusses how, throughout the tragedies of his life, Malcolm overcame them and grew up to help others.

Author Walter Dean Myers brought the world another wonderful children's book about Malcolm X titled *Malcolm X: A Fire Burning Brightly*. Published in 2003, this book centers on one of Malcolm's most famous quotes, "I believe in recognizing every human being as a human being, neither white, black, brown, nor red" to explain to children how Malcolm X stood up for equality of the African American race.[13]

Malcolm's Memorials and Tributes

In 1984, the site where Malcolm's first childhood home stood in Omaha, Nebraska, became a member on the National Register of Historic Places. Unfortunately, the actual house Malcolm and his family lived in right after his birth is no

---

[13] Amazon.com. (n.d.). [online] Available at:
https://www.amazon.com/Malcolm-X-Fire-Burning-Brightly/dp/0060562013/ref=asc_df_0060562013/?tag=hyprod-20&linkCode=df0&hvadid=312089887152&hvpos=1o2&hvnetw=g&hvrand=7587255418430059118&hvpone=&hvptwo=&hvqmt=&hvdev=c&hvdvcmdl=&hvlocint=&hvlocphy=9020205&hvtargid=pla-463067538852&psc=1.

longer standing. The owners of the house in 1965 tore it down without knowing its connection to Malcolm X.

Several major cities around the world, especially the ones where Malcolm lived and spoke, such as Harlem, New York, and Berkeley, California, celebrate Malcolm X's birthday, which is known as Malcolm X day. Celebrated on May 19, people fill this day with educational opportunities not only about Malcolm X but also about the civil rights movement. The first known Malcolm X day took place on May 19, 1971, in Washington, D.C. Since then, the celebration has grown, though the day is not considered any type of holiday, except for the cities which have created this date as a city-wide holiday, such as Berkeley.

In 1975, Lansing, Michigan, placed a historical marker on the site of Malcolm X's childhood home, where he spent many of his young years. The city has further honored Malcolm's legacy by establishing the El-Hajj Malik El-Shabazz Academy, located in the same building Malcolm X attended elementary school. As a public charter school, the El-Hajj Malik El-Shabazz Academy focuses more on African American history, heritage, and culture than the majority of other schools in the United States. The area established this school due to Malcolm X's belief that the younger African American generation needs to gain a better understanding of who they are and where their ancestors came from. For Malcolm X, this became one of his stronger focuses in his later life, especially his last few years, after the birth of his children. On top of the academy, many other schools have renamed their schools after Malcolm X, including schools in Madison, Wisconsin, and Newark, New Jersey. There are even colleges named after Malcolm X, such as the Malcolm X Liberation University in North Carolina, which was established four years after Malcolm's assassination.

In 2005, Malcolm X and Dr. Betty Shabazz Memorial and Educational Center had its grand opening. This center is located in the Audubon Ballroom, where Malcolm X was assassinated fifty years before the opening. The center opened on May 19, which would have been Malcolm's eightieth birthday. The mission for the center is to not only carry on the legacy of Malcolm X and his wife, but also to create a place with an educational focus where people can learn about the couple, their lives, and their beliefs. On top of this, the center focuses on creating a more advanced learning environment as Malcolm and his wife truly believed in the advanced education of children. Columbia University runs the museum and houses most of Malcolm X and his wife's documents in the museum archives. The center features interactive educational exhibits.

Most recently, Malcolm is remembered by American protesters in another way. While Malcolm has always been seen by some as a powerful and intelligent leader, on in which they idolized through their protesting, more Americans are viewing Malcolm in this light. Over the past few years, the Black Lives Matter movement has focused on changing the lives of African Americans. Black Lives Matter focuses on intervening against police brutality towards African Americans. While this movement has caused controversy over the years, it's also helped raise awareness to continued racism against African Americans by law enforcement.

As a global movement, many supporters of the Black Lives Matter movement cite the similarities between this movement and Malcolm X's stance against police brutality. As stated before, while he was a member of the Nation of Islam, Malcolm X believed African Americans should respond with violence when faced with violence. While the Black Lives Matter movement has never specifically stated African Americans should respond with violence when they are a target of violence. Many of the protest held by supports of the Black Lives Matter movement has broken out in violence, however, many other protests have been peaceful.

Both the violence and peaceful protesting of the Black Lives Matter movement has caused people to either blame or honor Malcolm X's legacy. Some people believe that the Black Lives Matter movement's reaction with violence stems from Malcolm X's beliefs on violence for violence but other people believe that the peaceful protests and the mission of the Black Lives Matter movement is honoring the legacy of Malcolm X. No matter what you believe, there is no denying that the similarity between the mission of intervening on police brutality against African Americans and Malcolm X's stance on African Americans coming together to stand up to police brutality by any means necessary. Because of this similarity, it's hard to deny that the Black Lives Matter movement doesn't honor the legacy of Malcolm X.

After reading this book, you probably have your thoughts about if the Black Lives Matter movement not only honors the legacy of Malcolm X in a positive and correct light. But, whatever feelings and thoughts people have towards the similarities of the Black Lives Matter movement and honoring Malcolm X's legacy, no one can deny the importance of Malcolm X in the Civil Rights Movement, in African American history, or in American history.

Even if you don't believe violence is the answer to violence, you can't deny the importance of Malcolm X's work as a leader, not only of the Nation of Islam but in the Civil Rights Movement and how his legacy needs to be honored. For over a decade, Malcolm X did whatever he felt was needed in order to help bring equality to the lives of African Americans. Malcolm X often put his own life on the line in order to fight for the injustices against the African American communities. With the molding from his childhood and those who influenced Malcolm X throughout his life, he did what he believed was right in order to better the lives of African Americans. Above all, no one can deny that when Malcolm X stated one of his most famous quotes, "If you're not ready to die for it, put the word 'freedom' out of your vocabulary" that he wasn't ready to die for what he believed in.[14] And for Malcolm X, he lived up to his quote as he did die fighting for what he believed in, which was freedom for African Americans.

[14] Malcolmx.com. (n.d.). Quotes – Malcolm X. [online] Available at:
https://www.malcolmx.com/quotes/.

Conclusion

Today, Malcolm X continues to be one of the most controversial civil rights activists, but he is also one of the most influential. Just like any other human being, which was all Malcolm X wanted to be treated as, he made mistakes, but this should never take away from everything Malcolm X accomplished through his life.

Over the last couple decades, Malcolm X's reputation has changed as more information about him emerges. While this initially started with the release of Alex Haley's *The Autobiography of Malcolm X* only a few short months after Malcolm's assassination, many people didn't read the book until many years later. When Malcolm passed away, his reputation remained very controversial because he never left the shadow of the angry black man of America. Only a year before his death, Malcolm X started to transform into the person his family saw him as, and during most of this time he traveled the world, where he not only met with other leaders of nations but also started to work towards understanding himself better.

Today, at least for those who look beyond the angry black man image, Malcolm X is a true icon of not only civil rights but human rights. Towards the end of his life, Malcolm X became more of a human rights activist as he wanted to see all races receive the same equal treatment. Through his pilgrimage to Mecca, Malcolm learned that all races can celebrate one cause or event, and he truly began to believe that this could happen on American soil. This opened Malcolm's eyes and soon he started to believe that things he had felt were impossible his whole life were truly possible. Throughout the remainder of his life, Malcolm would discuss how this moment led him to become the person he truly desired, not only for himself but for African Americans and any other person in the world who needed someone to look up to.

From a child whose family fell apart, to one of the most important civil rights leaders during the 1950s and 1960s, Malcolm X tried to create the world he felt he deserved as an adolescent. He didn't understand why people who reacted with violence towards African Americans because of their color of their skin should be treated with silent protests. Instead, Malcolm felt that they should receive the same treatment they handed out. The only hesitation Malcolm had with this view was with white children. Even though white people injured African American children through bombing a church during Sunday school or by spraying them with water during a demonstration, Malcolm couldn't justify harming children. Malcolm saw this as the children simply mimicking the adults who they needed to listen to and were told to respect. So, Malcolm blamed the adults for the behavior of white children.

While Malcolm X continues to be thought of as one of the most controversial figures during the civil rights movement, many feel he is simply misunderstood, even by people today. Several historians have investigated the life of Malcolm X, trying to understand what made Malcolm tick and why he felt so strongly about gaining complete freedom in any way possible when he also felt that African Americans would never truly gain freedom in the United States, so they needed to head back to Africa and create their community.

When looking at this while analyzing Malcolm's life, the answer can boil down to several reasons. First, even though Malcolm felt every African Americans were brainwashed by the white population or some other group, he also became brainwashed while living his life under the rules of the Nation of Islam. On top of this, people could view Malcolm was brainwashing others into believing what the Nation of Islam taught because of the amount of control he had over his followers.

A second reason is Malcolm's childhood. While Malcolm remained close with the majority of his brothers and sisters, even after the family split up in the late 1930s, Malcolm lived a traumatic childhood with the murder of his father and the slow mental decline of his mother. As a child, Malcolm began to feel like he truly mattered in a white -controlled world, but soon learned that just because of the color of his skin, he would always be seen as different. He wouldn't be able to become what he wanted to be because he was an African American. He started to notice that he would be viewed by whites, even the ones he felt cared about him, as less than human because of the color of his skin. For any young child and adolescent, these are memories that help mold the person into who they will become. There are always some pieces of us that we can never fully let go of.

No one can deny the intelligence and talent Malcolm possessed as a person. He held an amazing talent for public speaking, one which could draw in people and make them not only think about what Malcolm was saying but also attribute Malcolm's words to their own lives. Through learning about Malcolm X, a person learned about someone who felt passionately about his beliefs and would do anything in his power to create a better life for African Americans of his time and future generations. Like so many other civil rights activists, Malcolm X is a true hero of that era.

Bibliography

A History of Malcolm X. (n.d.). *Johnson Hinton: Malcolm X Became Famous Because of the Johnson Hinton Incident.* [online] Available at: https://ahistoryofmalcolmx.weebly.com/johnson-hinton.html.

Akinti, P. (2005). *Malcolm X insulted.* [online] the Guardian. Available at: https://www.theguardian.com/world/2005/may/26/usa.features11.

Aljazeera.com. (2018). *Malcolm X: From Nation of Islam to Black Power Movement.* [online] Available at: https://www.aljazeera.com/news/2018/02/malcolm-nation-islam-black-power-movement-180221085553908.html.

Shabazz, I. (2014). *Malcolm Little: The Boy Who Grew Up To Be Malcolm X.* Atheneum Books for Young Readers. Amazon.com. (n.d.). [online] Available at: https://www.amazon.com/Malcolm-Little-Boy-Grew-Become/dp/144241216X/ref=asc_df_144241216X/?tag=hyprod-20&linkCode=df0&hvadid=312105353883&hvpos=101&hvnetw=g&hvrand=7587255418430059118&hvpone=&hvptwo=&hvqmt=&hvdev=c&hvdvcmdl=&hvlocint=&hvlocphy=9020205&hvtargid=pla-618618041967&psc=1.

Myers, W. (2003). *Malcolm X: A Fire Burning Brightly.* Amistad. Amazon.com. (n.d.). [online] Available at: https://www.amazon.com/Malcolm-X-Fire-Burning-Brightly/dp/0060562013/ref=asc_df_0060562013/?tag=hyprod-

20&linkCode=dfo&hvadid=312089887152&hvpos=102&hvnet
w=g&hvrand=7587255418430059118&hvpone=&hvptwo=&hv
qmt=&hvdev=c&hvdvcmdl=&hvlocint=&hvlocphy=9020205&
hvtargid=pla-463067538852&psc=1.

Angeles, O. (2002). *Mecca 'made Malcolm X change.'* [online]
Telegraph.co.uk.   Available   at:
https://www.telegraph.co.uk/news/worldnews/middleeast/sa
udiarabia/1387524/Mecca-made-Malcolm-X-change.html.

Bath, P. (2015). *The Religious Life of Malcolm X - U.S. Studies
Online.*   [online]   Baas.ac.uk.   Available   at:
http://www.baas.ac.uk/usso/the-religious-life-of-malcolm-x/.

Black Lives Matter. (n.d.). Black Lives Matter: About Us.
[online] Available at: https://blacklivesmatter.com/about/.

Burnett, L. (2009). *Organization of Afro-American Unity
(OAAU)   1965.*   [online]   BlackPast.   Available   at:
https://www.blackpast.org/african-american-
history/organization-afro-american-unity-oaau-1965/.

Carson, C. (2018). *Malcolm X: The FBI File.* New York:
Skyhorse Publishing. Kindle Edition.

Cbsnews.com. (n.d.). *The Assassination of Malcolm X in
Photos: 50   Years   Later.*   [online]   Available   at:
https://www.cbsnews.com/pictures/the-assassination-of-
malcolm-x-50-years/.

DeCaro, Jr., L. (1998). *Malcolm and the Cross.* [online]
Google   Books.   Available   at:
https://books.google.com/books?id=sSYTCgAAQBAJ&printse
c=frontcover&dq=Malcolm+X&hl=en&sa=X&ved=0ahUKEwj
W4uXArrLgAhUCh-
AKHazUDiIQ6AEIRTAF#v=onepage&q=Malcolm%20X&f=fal
se.

Edwards, P. (2019). *This is the Telegram MLK Sent Malcolm X's wife After Her Husband's Assassination.* [online] Vox. Available at: https://www.vox.com/2015/2/21/8078739/mlk-malcolm-x-telegrams.

En.wikipedia.org. (n.d.). *Muslim Mosque, Inc..* [online] Available   at: https://en.wikipedia.org/wiki/Muslim_Mosque,_Inc.

En.wikipedia.org. (n.d.). *Organization of Afro-American Unity.*   [online]   Available   at: https://en.wikipedia.org/wiki/Organization_of_Afro-American_Unity.

En.wikipedia.org. (n.d.). *The Hate That Hate Produced.* [online]   Available   at: https://en.wikipedia.org/wiki/The_Hate_That_Hate_Produced.

Encyclopedia.com. (n.d.). *Malcolm X (1925–1965), Black Muslim Leader | Encyclopedia.com.* [online] Available at: https://www.encyclopedia.com/religion/legal-and-political-magazines/malcolm-x-1925-1965-black-muslim-leader.

Enisuoh, A. (n.d.). *The Nation of Islam (Black Muslims) | Socialist Alternative.* [online] Socialistalternative.org. Available at: https://www.socialistalternative.org/life-legacy-malcolm-x/nation-islam-black-muslims/.

Gardner, J. (2005). *Monthly Review | The Murder of Malcolm X.* [online] Monthly Review. Available at: https://monthlyreview.org/2005/02/01/the-murder-of-malcolm-x/.

Goalcast. (n.d.). *20 Malcolm X Quotes to Inspire You to Take Control of Your Life.* [online] Available at: https://www.goalcast.com/2018/10/03/malcolm-x-quotes/.

Hamilton, A. (2015). *Malcolm X: The Road to Revolution.* [online] Socialist Review. Available at: http://socialistreview.org.uk/399/malcolm-x-road-revolution.

Harris, C. (2002). *Malcolm X – Visionary, Activist, Family Man.* [online] Ilaam.net. Available at: http://www.ilaam.net/Opinions/MalcolmXVisionary.html.

Harris, J. (n.d.). *The Role of the Nation of Islam in the Civil Rights Movement | Study.com.* [online] Study.com. Available at: https://study.com/academy/lesson/the-role-of-the-nation-of-islam-in-the-civil-rights-movement.html.

HISTORY. (2009). *Malcolm X.* [online] Available at: https://www.history.com/topics/black-history/malcolm-x.

Historyisaweapon.com. (n.d.). *Malcolm X on Afro-American History.* [online] Available at: https://www.historyisaweapon.com/defcon1/malconafamhist.html.

Jones, R. (2015). Reclaiming Malcolm X. [online] Civilrightsmuseum.org. Available at: https://www.civilrightsmuseum.org/news/posts/reclaiming-malcolm-x.

Keyes, A. (2018). *Malcolm X Tells His Story in New Documentary Featuring Rarely and Never Before Seen Footage.* [online] Theroot.com. Available at: https://www.theroot.com/malcolm-x-tells-his-story-in-new-documentary-featuring-1823249920.

Lord, L., Thornton, J. and Bodipo-Memba, A. (1992). *The Legacy of Malcolm X: He Terrified Whites and Turned Negroes into African-Americans.* [online] Web.archive.org. Available at: https://web.archive.org/web/20120307010649/http://www.u

snews.com/usnews/culture/articles/921123/archive_018698
_5.htm.

Machi, A. (n.d.). *Malcolm X's Dedication to the Truth is Something to Which All Muslims Aspire | Aseel Machi.* [online] the Guardian. Available at: https://www.theguardian.com/commentisfree/2014/feb/21/malcolm-x-anniversary-legacy-islam-ideals-humility.

Malcolmx.com. (n.d.). *Quotes – Malcolm X.* [online] Available at: http://www.malcolmx.com/quotes/.

Malcolm X Legacy. (n.d.). *Biography.* [online] Available at: https://malcolmxlegacy.com/pages/about-malcolm.

Mamiya, L. (1999). *Malcolm X | Biography, Nation of Islam, Assassination, & Facts.* [online] Encyclopedia Britannica. Available at: https://www.britannica.com/biography/Malcolm-X.

Marable, M. (2011). *Malcolm X: A Life of Reinvention.* Penguin Books. Kindle Edition.

Massmoments.org. (n.d.). *Malcolm X Imprisoned.* [online] Available at: https://www.massmoments.org/moment-details/malcolm-x-imprisoned.html.

Melton, J. (1998). *Nation of Islam | History, Founder, Beliefs, & Facts.* [online] Encyclopedia Britannica. Available at: https://www.britannica.com/topic/Nation-of-Islam.

Michaud, J. (2011). *Malcolm X and Elijah Muhammad.* [online] The New Yorker. Available at: https://www.newyorker.com/books/double-take/malcolm-x-and-elijah-muhammad.

Muhammad, E. (1965). *The Muslim Program - NOI.org Official Website.* [online] NOI.org Official Website. Available at: https://www.noi.org/muslim-program/.

NOI.org Official Website. (n.d.). *Brief History on Origin of the Nation of Islam - NOI.org Official Website.* [online] Available at: https://www.noi.org/noi-history/.

NYCgo.com. (n.d.). *The Malcolm X and Dr. Betty Shabazz Memorial & Educational Center.* [online] Available at: https://www.nycgo.com/arts-culture/the-malcolm-x-and-dr.-betty-shabazz-memorial-educational-center.

Nytimes.com. (n.d.). *MALCOLM X SCORES U.S. AND KENNEDY; Likens Slaying to 'Chickens Coming Home to Roost' Newspapers Chided.* [online] Available at: https://www.nytimes.com/1963/12/02/archives/malcolm-x-scores-us-and-kennedy-likens-slaying-to-chickens-coming.htm.

Patel, D. (2017). *Malcolm X: If You Don't Stand for Something You Will Fall for Anything.* Kindle Edition.

Revolvy.com. (n.d.). "Muslim Mosque, Inc." on Revolvy.com. [online] Available at: https://www.revolvy.com/page/Muslim-Mosque%2C-Inc.

Robinson, T. (2014). *Malcolm X.* [online] Google Books. Available at: https://books.google.com/books?id=b7J7AgAAQBAJ&printsec=frontcover&dq=Malcolm+X&hl=en&sa=X&ved=0ahUKEwjW4uXArrLgAhUCh-AKHazUDiIQ6AEIMDAB#v=onepage&q=Malcolm%20X&f=false.

Rummel, J. and Wanger, H. (2005). *Malcolm X.* [online] Google Books. Available at:

https://books.google.com/books?id=8auDbJtuOAsC&pg=PA1
4&lpg=PA14&dq=Gohannases+Malcolm+X&source=bl&ots=
Qgbo5RGSwR&sig=ACfU3U2fNwk7yA_S-
g19TJCzJqxwsAWoAg&hl=en&sa=X&ved=2ahUKEwj23aGjnb
LgAhXHnOAKHeBKAX8Q6AEwB3oECAIQAQ#v=onepage&q
=Gohannases%20Malcolm%20X&f=false.

Ryan, S.J., P. (2014). *One Pilgrim's Progress: When Malcolm
X became El-Hajj Malik El-Shabazz.* [online] America
Magazine. Available at:
https://www.americamagazine.org/issue/one-pilgrims-
progress.

Spellman, A. (2001). *Interview with Malcolm X.* [online]
Hartford-hwp.com. Available at: http://www.hartford-
hwp.com/archives/45a/388.html.

Stanley, T. (2015). *Malcolm X's Assassination Robbed the
World of a Muslim Civil Rights Visionary.* [online]
Telegraph.co.uk. Available at:
https://www.telegraph.co.uk/history/11422926/Malcolm-Xs-
assassination-robbed-the-world-of-a-Muslim-civil-rights-
visionary.html.

Teachingamericanhistory.org. (n.d.). *A Summing Up: Louis
Lomax interviews Malcolm X | Teaching American History.*
[online] Available at:
http://teachingamericanhistory.org/library/document/a-
summing-up-louis-lomax-interviews-malcolm-x/.

The Economist. (n.d.). *What He Might Have Become.* [online]
Available at: https://www.economist.com/books-and-
arts/2011/04/07/what-he-might-have-become

Tristam, P. (2018). *Malcolm X in Mecca When Malcolm
Embraced True Islam and Abandoned Racial Separatism.*

[online] ThoughtCo. Available at: https://www.thoughtco.com/malcom-x-in-mecca-2353496.

Ushistory.org. (n.d.). *Malcolm X and the Nation of Islam* [ushistory.org]. [online] Available at: http://www.ushistory.org/us/54h.asp.

Web-static.nypl.org. (2005). *NYPL, Malcolm X: A Search for Truth.* [online] Available at: http://web-static.nypl.org/exhibitions/malcolmx/index.html.

Watch The Yard. (n.d.). *Did You Know That Malcolm X's Wife, Dr. Betty Shabazz, Was A Member Of Delta Sigma Theta?.* [online] Available at: https://www.watchtheyard.com/deltas/malcolm-x-wife-betty-shabazz-delta-sigma-theta/.

X, M. and Haley, A. (1965). *The Autobiography of Malcolm X.* New York: Random House Publishing Group. Kindle Edition.

X, M. (2018). *Malcolm X: The Pilgrimage to Makkah - IslamiCity.* ·[online] Islamicity.org. Available at: https://www.islamicity.org/6279/malcolm-x-the-pilgrimage-to-makkah/.

X, M. (2011). *The End of White Supremacy: Four Speeches.* Skyhorse. Kindle Edition.

YouTube. (2017). The Hate That Hate Produced (1959) | Malcom X First TV Appearance. [online] Available at: https://www.youtube.com/watch?v=BsYWD2EqavQ.

Zelenkova, B. (2015). *The Life and Struggles of Malcolm X.* [online] Ethnologist.info. Available at: https://ethnologist.info/section/world-resorts/north-america/the-life-of-malcolm-x/.

Manufactured by Amazon.ca
Bolton, ON

25017442R00074